GW00857896

Migrating to Windows 8.1

For computer users without a touch screen, coming from XP, Vista or Windows 7

By Dr. Andy Williams

http://ezseonews.com

Version 2.0

Published on 9th January 2014

Table of Contents

What people are saying about this book *1*

DISCLAIMER AND TERMS OF USE AGREEMENT *2*

Introduction to Windows 8 ....*3*

How to use this book *4*

Starting Windows 8 - A quick tour of the Windows 8 interface *5*

    The lock screen **5**

    The start screen **6**

    Metro apps Vs Windows applications **6**

    To the Desktop! **8**

    The desktop has hotspots **10**

        The bottom left hotspot 10
        The top left hotspot 11
        The top right hotspot 14
        The bottom right hotspot 14

The lock screen *15*

    How to disable the lock screen **16**

    Lock screen apps **17**

        Setting up lock screen apps 17

    Changing the lock screen picture **21**

The login screen *22*

Login options *23*

    Using a picture password **25**

    Using a PIN **25**

        Booting Windows 8 with Num Lock ON 25

The start screen *26*

    Working with tiles **27**

        Re-arranging tiles 27
        Start screen command menu 27
        How to add tiles for applications you want included in the start menu...........28

    Naming a group of apps **30**

    Pin a folder to the start screen **32**

Metro apps 33

    The Metro app store 33

    To install a Metro app 36

    Install app updates 38

    Uninstalling an app 40

    App commands 41

    Closing apps 42

Searching from the start screen 45

Where is the old start button? 47

    Adding the old start button back 47

The Charms bar 51

    Search 52

    Share 54

    Start 58

    Devices 59

    Settings 61

PC settings 66

    PC and devices 67

        Lock Screen 68

        Display 68

        Bluetooth 68

        Devices 68

        Mouse and touchpad 68

        Typing 68

        Corners and edges 68

        Power and sleep 69

        Autoplay 69

        PC Info 69

    Accounts 71

        Your Account 71

        Sign-In Options 71

        Other Accounts 71

    SkyDrive 72

        File Storage 72

        Camera Roll 72

Sync Settings 72

Metered Connections 73

Search and apps **74**

Search 74

Share 75

Notifications 75

App sizes 76

Defaults 77

Privacy **79**

General 79

Location 80

Webcam 80

Microphone 80

Other devices 81

Network **82**

Connections 82

Flight Mode 82

Proxy 83

Homegroup 83

Workplace 83

Time and Language **84**

Date and Time 84

Region and language 84

Ease of Access **85**

Narrator 85

Magnifier 85

High Contrast 86

Keyboard 86

Mouse 86

Other Options 86

Update and Recovery **87**

Windows Update 87

File History 87

Recovery 87

File Explorer *89*

Sky Drive *93*

How to *95*

Accessing the Windows 8 control panel **96**

Windows Update Settings **97**

How to set up a Homegroup 99

    Sharing in a Homegroup 100

Scroll through open apps 102

Add a Windows user 103

Note about account types 103

    Microsoft account or local account? 104

Delete a Windows user 105

Printing in Windows 8 107

    Printing from traditional Windows applications 107

    Printing from Windows File Explorer 107

    Printing from Metro apps 107

Take a screenshot 109

    The Window "Snipping Tool" 109

Create a slideshow of your photos 112

    Slideshow from File Explorer 112

Searching in Windows 8 115

    Search Shortcuts 115

    Manually switching search mode 115

Advanced searches in Windows 8's File Explorer 116

    Using Search Tools in Explorer 117

    Search by file extension 119

    Using Boolean operators to search 120

Snapping apps and applications to the sidebar 121

    Snapping Metro apps 121

    Snapping desktop applications 124

How to open two copies of File Explorer 126

How to turn Airplane/Flight mode On/Off 127

How to open the Windows Task Manager 129

How to shut down, restart or put your computer to sleep 130

    Shut down from the Desktop 131

    Creating Desktop icons to shut down 132

Manually check for windows updates 135

Change the Desktop wallpaper & create themes 136

View basic information about your computer 138

Zooming with CTRL + mouse wheel 140

Changing the time zone 141

Change your account picture **142**

Connecting to a WIFI **143**

Change the Windows 8 language **145**

Using dual monitors **148**
   The position of the second monitor in "Extend" mode 148

Reinstall Windows 8 .... **151**

How to refresh your computer **152**

Emails - setting up an email address in Windows Mail **153**
   Adding a second email address to Windows Mail 154
   Manually setting up an email account 155
   Change email account name in Windows Mail 157
   Getting notifications when new Mail arrives 158

Windows 8 keyboard shortcuts *159*

Where to go from here *161*

A cheat sheet **161**

"How to" suggestions? **161**

My Other Kindle Books **162**
   Kindle Publishing – Format, Publish & Promote your Books on Kindle 162
   WordPress For Beginners 163
   CSS For Beginners 163

What people are saying about this book

"What Microsoft should buy and give away now to drive sales

Desktop computing since 1981, I've almost always found it useful to upgrade as new versions of software have come out. But I sure don't want to have to take a course to do it (I'm not tech-savvy, I write for a living). This very helpful, nicely illustrated guide is what Microsoft should simply buy from Dr. Williams and give away to drive Win-8 sales. Once word spreads that a new operating system is "hard to learn," the first instinct of the herd is to stick with what they know, Win-7. Having a book like this on hand eases the decision to upgrade to Win-8". **Geewhizicist**

"Dr. Williams I must thank you! I just recently purchased a new laptop with the Windows 8 OS. The new laptop is sitting in my closet because I am very comfortable with Windows 7 and Windows8 is somewhat intimidating. Now I have the skills to start using my new laptop. The information is well documented and the instructions are even better than the MS instructional manual. My hat goes off to you for this wonderful tutorial!" **Doc Rick**

"I like the book for its simple and direct explanations tat are easy to understand. Gives you a big assist from what the dolts at Microsoft provided upon purchase. It showed me a few of the mysteries that Windows 8 brings as well as a way to use the old start interface". **Robert Metras**

"If you already know how to use a computer and want to get to the nitty gritty of Windows 8, this is the best $3 you'll spend! I have read through it and will sit down in front of my computer and go through it again. I was clueless about Windows 8 and now feel more comfortable". **William E. Haines**

"You need a new PC, you go to the shop thinking you know all about it and find yourself faced with an interface that makes little sense to you. Why, Microsoft, why? I am a big fan of Dr Andy's writing but I am especially pleased by this book. Essential reading for anybody "upgrading" to Windows 8". **Pearson Brown**

"If like me you and technolololology have an awkward relationship, then you probably don't respond well to instructions provided by manufacturers, that's if you even try to look at them. This is a great book for anyone making the migration to wondows 8. Everything is explained nice and easy, and everything is illustrated. I recommend this book". **Michael Finlayson**

DISCLAIMER AND TERMS OF USE AGREEMENT

Introduction to Windows 8

Windows 8 is probably the least intuitive Windows operating system (OS) I have ever used.   The main reason for this, I believe, is that Microsoft wanted to create a single operating system that could be used on two entirely different types on device – namely tablets and smartphones, which are touch-screen, and desktop/laptop computers that are not (at least not the majority).   To me, Windows 8 feels like two different operating systems that have been cobbled together and forced to work together.

If, like me, you are using a non-touch screen, then some of the features of Windows 8 just seem a little bizarre.   On touch screens things do make a lot more sense and I guess that is where Microsoft believes computers are heading.   With more and more computer manufacturers creating touch enabled screens, prices will drop, and I imagine we'll end up with most laptops and even desktops having touch-enabled monitors.   However, until that time, we traditional PC users are going to have to make the transition to an operating system that wasn't really optimized for the computers we presently work on.

I wrote this book to help make the shift to Windows 8 a little less painful for those working on a non-touch screen computer.   While I cannot cover the whole operating system, I have done my best to cover the things that beginners often get most confused about.

The book starts with a quick tour of the Windows 8 interface, and I suggest you go through this first.   After that, we'll go through the main features of Windows 8 and the important settings and customisations you should know about.   I've included an extensive "how to" section that will answer a lot of the commonly asked questions. We'll finish the book with a complete list of keyboard shortcuts that help to get things done quicker.

Before we start, I'd like to mention one more thing. With previous versions of Windows, keyboard shortcuts were something that could be used as an option.   With Windows 8, keyboard shortcuts have become more of an essential way of getting things done.   You can use Windows 8 without them, but you'll lose most of your hair trying.

How to use this book

To get the most out of this book, I'd recommend reading it while you sit in front of your computer, Windows 8 open in front of you. Try the stuff as you go through the pages. That way, you'll get to explore all of the main areas of Windows 8 and start getting used to those keyboard shortcuts.

Starting Windows 8 - A quick tour of the Windows 8 interface

We are going to be looking in detail at how to get things done in Windows 8, but before we do, I thought it would be beneficial to take a whirlwind tour of the interface so that we can give names to the various bits we'll be discussing later. Microsoft seem to have developed a small vocabulary specific to the new operating system, so it's important that we all know what each feature is called, right?

The lock screen

Whenever you start, reboot, lock, or wake up Windows 8, the screen you'll see is the **lock screen**.

Clicking the screen with your mouse will remove this display and you'll be presented with the password prompt.   You enter your password - if you've set one up - (click your user profile if you haven't), and then you'll land on the **start screen**.

The start screen

The start screen displays a number of tiles that represent applications on your computer.

Clicking any of these tiles opens the application.

Metro apps Vs Windows applications

Now, there are two types of applications here - **Metro apps** and **Windows applications**.

Windows applications are the typical ones you have always run on Windows. They run inside their own window and have a title bar with minimize, maximize and close buttons in the top right corner:

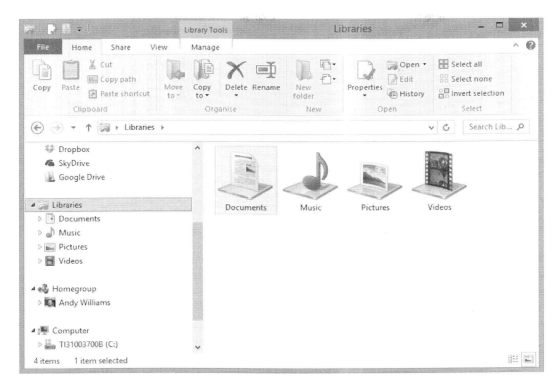

Metro apps are the new Windows 8 applications that appear to be designed more for tablets and touch screens, than desktop and laptops.   These apps run full screen and don't have minimize, maximize or close buttons in the top right corner.   Here is a screenshot of a finance Metro app:

What you see in the screenshot takes up the full monitor real estate.   Notice the absence of maximize, minimize and close buttons.

OK, back to your start screen.

To the Desktop!

On the start screen, you'll see a tile that represents your Desktop.

Click that tile to take you to your desktop.

Another way you can access the desktop from the start screen is to press the Escape key on your keyboard.

Windows keyboards also have a special "Windows" key.

 Pressing this key from the start screen will also take you to the desktop.

Most of the Windows 8 keyboard shortcuts use this key with another.

For example, pressing the "Windows key + D", will take you to your Windows desktop from any screen, be it the start screen, or from a Metro app.   Think of this combination as your failsafe way back to the desktop if you ever get lost.

OK, go to your desktop now.   For this you can click the desktop tile, press the ESCAPE key on your keyboard, or press the Windows button (note that Windows + D isn't needed from the start screen, but will still work).

In the original version of Windows 8, there was no Start Menu on the bottom left:

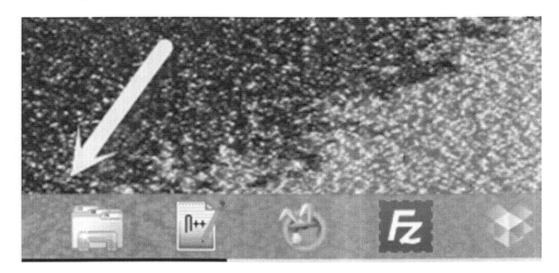

That's because the start menu we've just seen was supposed to replace the start button.   However, after a lot of complaints, Microsoft added a Start Menu to Windows 8.1.

The button is a simple Windows logo, unlike the Start Menus of the past.   However, before you rejoice at the Start Menu in Windows 8.1, there is something you need to know.   Clicking it takes you to the Start Screen we saw earlier, and not to the familiar menu system of previous Windows versions.

For those users that want a more familiar Start Menu, I'll show you later how to get one on Windows 8.1 with all the functionality you are used to.

The desktop has hotspots

The four corners of the screen represent hotspots.

The bottom left hotspot

Move your mouse into the bottom left corner.   In the original Windows 8 release, a popup preview of the Start Screen appeared:

This has been replaced in Windows 8.1 by the new start button, so this preview is no longer visible.   Instead you just see the start button highlighted:

Clicking this takes you to the Start Screen.

You can also access the start screen by pressing the "Windows" key on your keyboard.

The lower left corner of the screen also has another secret.   If you right-click in this corner, a popup menu appears:

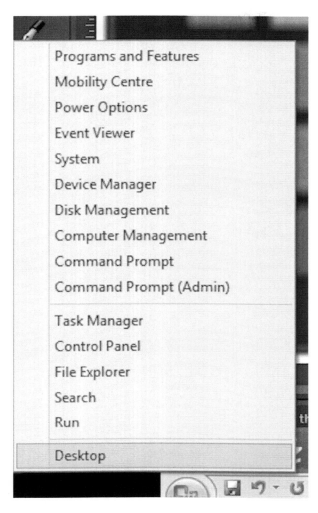

Programs and Features

Mobility Centre

Power Options

Event Viewer

System

Device Manager

Disk Management

Computer Management

Command Prompt

Command Prompt (Admin)

Task Manager

Control Panel

File Explorer

Search

Run

Desktop

This menu gives you access to a lot of system areas.

The top left hotspot

OK, now move your mouse to the top left of the screen.   Depending on whether you have anything open or not, you may or may not see anything.   I have some Metro apps open, so this is what I see:

Windows 8 shows a screenshot from one of the open Metro apps.

If you have more than one Metro app open, you will still only see the one screenshot. However, once you have that image showing on your screen, move your mouse straight down the left side of the display and the **Switch List** opens up, showing all Metro apps that are open:

You can right-click any app in this switch list to open a popup menu, allowing you to close the App, "snap left" or "snap right".

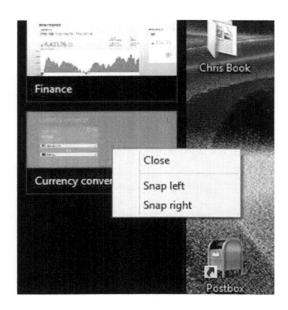

Snapping an App left or right attaches a smaller version of the app to the right or left sidebar:

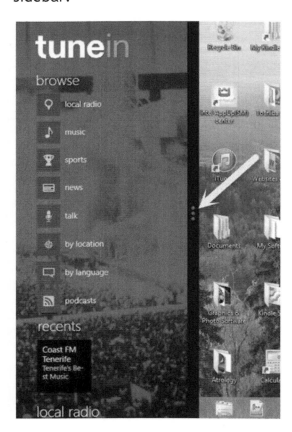

Notice the three circles half way down the divider (arrow in the screenshot).

You can drag that divider across to the right to increase the amount of space given to the snapped app. If you drag it back to the left, then the app becomes "unsnapped" from the sidebar.

NOTE: You can scroll through open Metro apps using the keyboard shortcut: **Windows Key + Tab**. Just keep tabbing until you highlight the one you want to run, and then release the keys to open it.

The top right hotspot

OK, now move your mouse up to the top right corner of the screen.

The white icons of the **Charms bar** appear on a transparent background. Move your mouse vertically down the right side of the screen and the Charms bar changes to a black background:

This is called the **Charms bar**, and we can access a lot of Windows 8 features from here.

By the way, if you find that moue manoeuvre a little difficult, you can also open the Charms bar using the keyboard shortcut: **Windows key + C** (this one is easy to remember as **Windows Key + C**harms).

The bottom right hotspot

The bottom right hotspot also opens the Charms bar.

OK, that's a brief tour of the Windows 8 interface. Let's now look at some of the main features in more detail.

14

The lock screen

Whenever you start your computer, reboot it, wake it up from "hibernation", or lock it, the lock screen is the one that shows. The lock screen is customizable, to a certain extent, and is designed to provide some basic information while protecting the device from unauthorized access.

This screen displays the date and time, WIFI and battery status, plus notifications from any "lock screen apps" that you have configured. We'll look at those later.

The background image you see on the lock screen is customizable, and we'll see how to change that later.

Clicking the mouse anywhere on the lock screen will remove it and take you to the login screen, from where you login to Windows 8.

How to disable the lock screen

If you are using a tablet, then the lock screen is fairly intuitive.   However, for PC users, it just adds another mouse click before you can start using your computer. You can disable this screen if you want to, but it requires a registry hack.   Rather than describe the hack here, there is an excellent article on this topic on the HowToGeek website:

http://www.howtogeek.com/134620/how-to-disable-the-lock-screen-on-windows-8-without-using-group-policy/

Lock screen apps

The lock screen can include information from some of the Metro apps on your computer.

For example, if you use the Windows 8 Calendar App for storing appointments, you can set this up as a lock screen app so that pending appointments are shown for the day directly on the lock screen itself. Or perhaps you use the Windows 8 mail program and want to show recent email messages that need your attention. You can configure 7 lock screen apps in total; with one being designated as the "details" app (this shows more detailed information from its respective App).

Setting up lock screen apps

We specify the lock screen apps in the PC Settings section of Windows 8.

We can get there in a number of different ways:

1. Move your mouse to the top right of the screen, then vertically down to display the charms bar (or press **Windows Key + C**). Click on **Settings**, and then select **Change PC Settings** at the bottom.

2. Press the keyboard shortcut **Windows Key + I** to open the Setting menu, and then select **Change PC Settings** at the bottom.

Once you have the PC settings screen open, you'll see the Personalize options are open on the right. The large image at the top is the lock screen, and clicking that image will take you to the **lock screen preview** screen (you can also get here by clicking the **PC and devices** menu item on the left).

Lock screen preview

11:08
Wednesday 8 January

Browse

Play a slide show on the lock screen
Off

At the top, you can select the lock screen image you want t use.

Lower down on the right of the screen, you'll see the lock screen apps section:

Lock-screen applications

Choose applications to run in the background and show quick status and notifications, even when your screen is locked

Choose an application to display detailed status

Choose an app to show alarms

Camera

Swipe down on the lock screen to use the camera

Off

The 7 icons in the row above represent the 7 apps you can have feeding information to your lock screen. The + symbol at the end allows me to add an app to that 7th position as I haven't defined one yet. Clicking on any of the app icon opens up a selector for choosing an app for that position. The selector looks like this:

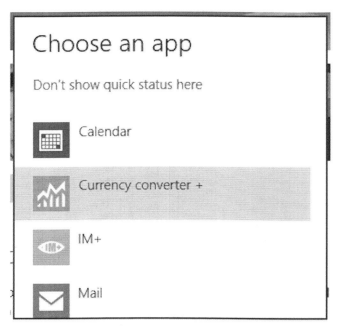

Simply scroll through the apps and select the ones you want for each position.

Under the row of 7 icons is one on its own. This one allows you to define an app that will provide more detailed information on your lock screen. I don't personally use the Mail or Calendar apps built into Windows 8, but if you do, then these might be logical choices for this coveted position.

19

Once you have set up your lock screen apps, press the **Windows Key + L** to display your lock screen.   You may or may not notice much difference.   This will depend on whether your chosen apps have any notifications for you.

Click anywhere on the Lock screen to bring up your login screen.

Changing the lock screen picture

You can change the picture that shows on the locks screen as follows:

Windows Key + I

Select "**Change PC Settings**" at the bottom of the bar.

On the PC Settings screen, select "**PC and devices**".

You'll now see a large image showing the current lock screen, with a row of smaller images underneath it.   You can choose any of these images, or click the browse button to find a different image on your hard disk.   This will then be used as your lock screen picture.   Whenever you change the image, you can quickly view your lock screen using the keyboard shortcut:

Windows Key + L

The login screen

What you see here will depend on how you set up Windows 8 when you installed it, or if you have customized it since installation.

When you first install Windows 8, it asks you to create a Microsoft account (formerly called a Windows Live account), or login with an existing one. This becomes your Windows 8 login password. Any customizations you make in Windows are then synced to your Microsoft account. If you have other Windows 8 devices (tablet, PC etc), you can use that same Microsoft account on all of them so your settings and customizations are synced between all devices.

It is possible to set up Windows 8 as a local account (which does not sync with a Microsoft account), although there will be some limitations.

If you do not have a password set up, you'll just see your Avatar. Click it to enter Windows 8.

If you have a password, PIN or Picture password set up, enter those to access Windows 8.

OK, let's now look at how to change the log-in type.

Login options

Once you are through the lock screen, you are taken to the login screen.

You can set this up to use either a password, a pin or an image.   You can change the sign-in method from the PC Settings.   The easiest way to get there is to use the keyboard shortcut:

Windows Key + I to open the Setting menu, then select **Change PC Settings** at the bottom.

For sign-in options, click on the **Accounts** item in the list on the left.   Your account will be shown on the right.   On the left, click **Sign-in options**.

Password

A strong password helps keep your account more secure

Change

Picture password

For best results, set up a picture password on the display you use to sign in to your PC

Add

PIN

Sign in quickly with a four-digit number

Change   Remove

Password policy

Password required when waking this PC from sleep

Change

The first option lets you change your password.

The second option lets you create a picture password.

The third option allows you to create a PIN. I am using a PIN on my own computer, so you may see a slightly different screen. I can change my PIN or remove it altogether (which would then default my sign-in back to the password).

The final option is the **Password Policy**. This allows you to switch off the password when waking up your computer. If you use a password on your machine, then you probably do not want to change this option, or anyone will be able to wake your computer.

Using a picture password

This is really only useful for those with touch screen devices. It allows you to choose a photo on your computer and assign gestures such as lines, circles and taps to the picture. The size, position and direction of your gestures then become your sign in "picture password".

Using a PIN

A PIN is a four-digit code made up of numbers. It represents a quick way to access your computer, though many computers don't boot up with the NUM Lock on, meaning an extra key press is needed, so bear that in mind (and check your computer).

Windows 8 will ignore any Bios settings for Num Lock during boot, so the only way to fix this is with a registry hack.

Booting Windows 8 with Num Lock ON

Only try this if you comfortable editing the registry.

Also, I cannot guarantee this will work for you. I have heard reports from some people that this fix works to begin with; then later stops working.

OK, to make your computer boot with the NUM Lock on, you need to edit a registry entry.

Press **Windows Key + R**

Type regedit and click OK.

Navigate to:

HKEY_USERS\.DEFAULT\Control Panel\Keyboard

Right click the entry **InitialKeyboardIndicators** and select Modify.

NOTE: Make a record of the value of this key before altering it. This way you can always change it back if it causes problems on your computer.

Now, here is where I have seen instructions online that did not work for me. A lot of websites say to change the value to 2. Many say change it from 0 to 2. Well mine didn't start out at 0 and changing it to 2 actually caused problems on my machine.

My **InitialKeyboardIndicators** value was 2147483648 and I changed it to 2147483650. Num Lock is now on when I get to the login screen.

The start screen

Once you login to Windows 8, the **start screen** is the first screen you see.

The Windows start screen is supposed to replace the old start button. Even so, it's a huge leap of faith and you have to totally rethink the way you find your applications. I can now honestly say though, that the start screen has become a favourite feature for me; it really is extremely powerful.

As you can see from the screenshot above, the start screen is made up of "tiles". Some of these tiles are large and others are small.

Several of the tiles are simply "icons" used to open applications, whereas others are "live tiles" that display some current information from the app they represent. Live tiles are only available for Metro apps though not all Metro apps.

Here is a live tile for a currency conversion app I installed:

The live tile tells me the current exchange rate for a currency I am interested in. If I click that live tile, just like any other tile, it will open the application.

Not surprisingly, you can customize the start screen by adding the apps you want, removing those you don't, reorganizing the tiles, and even change the background image and colours if you want to.

Working with tiles

Re-arranging tiles

To re-arrange tiles, you simple drag and drop them to the location you want them.

Start screen command menu

You can make the tiles large or small by right-clicking on them.   A commands menu appears at the bottom. On the left of this menu, you can see:

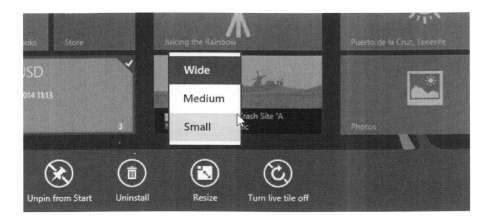

Unpin from Start - This will remove the tile from your start screen without uninstalling it.   You can always add the tile back later if you decide you want it there.

Uninstall - This will uninstall the application from your computer.

Resize – This gives you the option of changing the tile size.

Turn live tile off - This option will only be visible for live tiles.   If you don't want the application to update the tile, you can turn live notifications off.   This effectively makes the tile an application icon.

To the far right on this same commands bar, you have another option:

This button allows you to customize the Start Screen, moving items, grouping them and adding titles to your groups.

From the Start screen, you can scroll through the apps using the scroll bar at the bottom of the display, or by using a mouse wheel. You can also just start typing the name of the application that you want to find and the screen reverts to the search page which shows any matching apps for the text you have just entered.

How to add tiles for applications you want included in the start menu

There are several ways to add tiles for frequently used applications. One way is to press the keyboard shortcut, "**Windows Key + Q**" to bring up the search screen. You could also just bring up the Start screen by pressing the Windows key.

Just start typing the name of the app you want to pin to the start screen. The apps matching the text you have just typed will appear in the search results. Right click on the application and a popup menu appears:

Notice the option to also pin the app to the taskbar (the taskbar is the bar found on the desktop, usually at the bottom of the screen). This is useful for quick access to frequently used applications.

There are also options to uninstall, open in a new window, run as administrator, or open file location.

Side note: You can also pin applications to the start menu from Windows File Explorer.   Right-click on the program file in File Explorer and select **Pin to Start** from the popup menu.

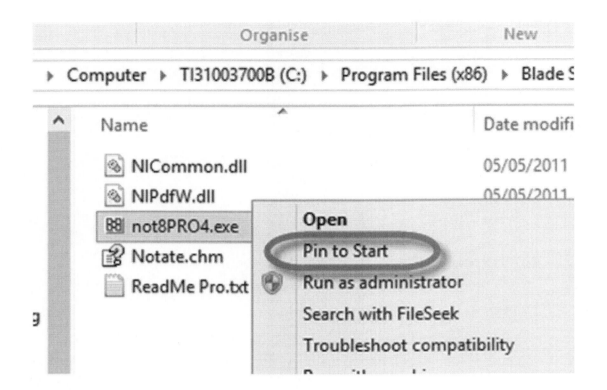

Naming a group of apps

The tiles on the start screen are organised into groups. One of the things that can help make it easier to find items is to give your groups identifiable names.

To do that, bring up the start screen (press the **Windows Key**) and right click somewhere on the background.

The Customize button appears in the bottom right of the screen. Click it.

You can now click into the titles of the groups and edit them:

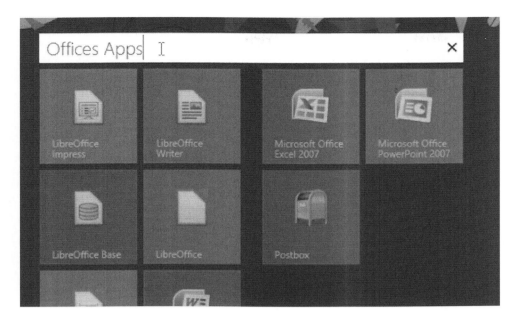

The name of the Group will now appear above that group in the start screen:

Pin a folder to the start screen

You can pin any folder to the start screen.

For example, I often have to open a folder on my computer that contains all of my newsletters for a website I run. To pin this folder to the start screen, I first need to navigate to the folder using File Explorer, and then right-click on the folder:

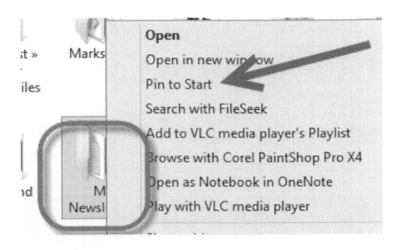

There is an option in the popup menu to **Pin to Start**.

This places the new tile on the far right of your start screen. You can now drag and drop it to wherever you want it displayed.

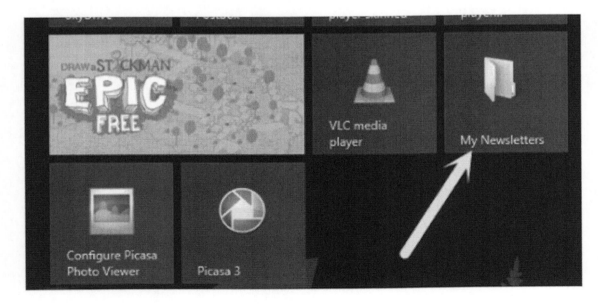

Clicking on a tile that represents a folder will open up that folder in File Explorer.

32

Metro apps

Metro apps are the touch-screen-friendly applications built into Windows 8. That doesn't mean you cannot use them on your desktop, because you can.

More and more software is being released in two forms - as a Metro app AND as a classic Windows application. From what I've seen though, the Metro versions tend to have fewer features than the full desktop version. For this reason, whenever there is a desktop version of a Metro app (e.g. Skype, Evernote), then I'll always use the desktop version.

A new feature of Windows 8 is the Metro app store, which is accessible directly from the start screen.

The Metro app store

Although this is called a "store", there are a lot of really cool free apps as well, just like Apple's App Store and Android's Google Play Store. You can access the App store in Windows 8 by clicking the store tile in the start screen.

Clicking that tile opens the App Store:

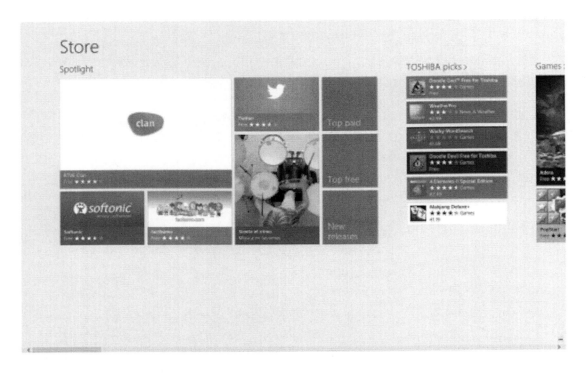

Your store may look a little different depending on your computer, but basically there will be groups of apps that you can browse though.

The apps in the store are grouped on the home screen, so you have games, photo, music and video, productivity, and so on.

If you right-click the background of the App Store, a command bar appears at the top giving thee options:

Home - will take you back to the home screen of the App Store.

Your apps - will take you to a screen that lists the apps you currently have installed.

Your Account – Takes you to your account details where you can set up payment methods, change user and enter redeem codes you might have.

You can search the App store by scrolling across the home screen (scroll bar along the bottom or by using the mouse wheel), and drilling down into anything you find interesting.   You can also search if you know what you are looking for.

To search, you just start typing in the search box located top right.

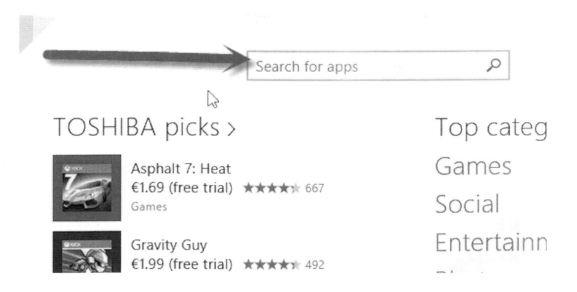

Any matches will appear underneath the search box, so click on the one that makes sense (or hit the return key on your keyboard).   The matches will then appear in the main app store area on the left of the screen.

To install a Metro app

Click to get more information about an app, including an overview, details and reviews (if any).   If the application is free, you can install it with a single mouse click.

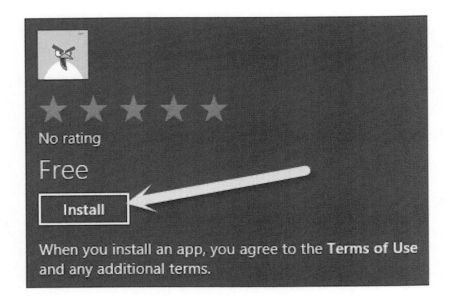

If it is a paid app, then you may get the option to download a trial version as well as a direct purchase.

To buy an App, you need to be logged into Windows with a Microsoft account (set up with your payment option).

Install app updates

When updates are available for the apps you have installed, you'll see a number on the app store tile.

Open the app store by clicking on the tile.

You'll see a link in the top right which indicates how many updates are available.

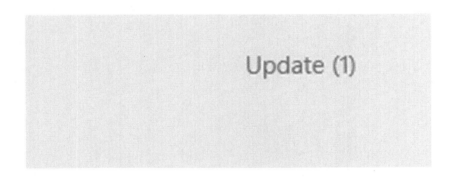

Click the link.

You will see a list of all apps that need updating at the top of the screen.   They will each have a check mark (tick), next to them to indicate an update is pending.

At the bottom, there is a command bar:

You can select/deselect individual app to update by clicking them with the left mouse button. Alternatively, if you want to update all apps that have updates available, click "**Select all**" in the command bar.

Once you have selected the apps to update, click the **Install** button.

This will then install all updates accordingly.

Uninstalling an app

To uninstall a Metro app, first locate it in the start screen.

Press the **Windows Key** to access the start screen and then start typing the name of the app.

When you find the app you're looking for, right-click on it.

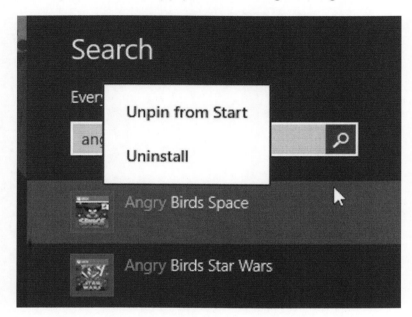

You'll get a menu that allows you to unpin it from the Start screen, and Uninstall it.

Click the **Uninstall** button to remove the App from your computer.

If you just want to remove it from your start screen, click the **Unpin from Start** instead.

App commands

App commands appear on the command bar and are specific to the app that has the focus.   You can access the app commands by right-clicking on the background of the app somewhere, or by using the keyboard shortcut, "**Windows Key + Z**".

For example, in the Music App, here is the main part of the command bar:

The weather app that I have installed has an upper and lower command bar:

Upper:

Lower:

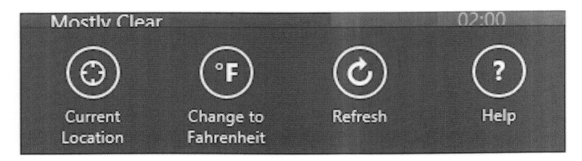

As you can see, the commands found in the command bar are the equivalent of traditional menu systems in Windows desktop applications.   The items displayed in the command bar for any given app will depend on the app itself, and will be the most important actions for that particular app.

Closing apps

Closing apps is something that many new Windows 8 users struggle with.   I mean, in every other Windows version since the beginning, there is a File menu with an exit option AND a red square with a cross in it located at the top right corner of the open window.   Metro apps don't have this.

To close a Metro app, you can either press ALT + F4, or use a more touch-friendly procedure of dragging the screen to the bottom of the display.   To do this, move your mouse to the top of the App screen so that the cursor changes to a small hand.

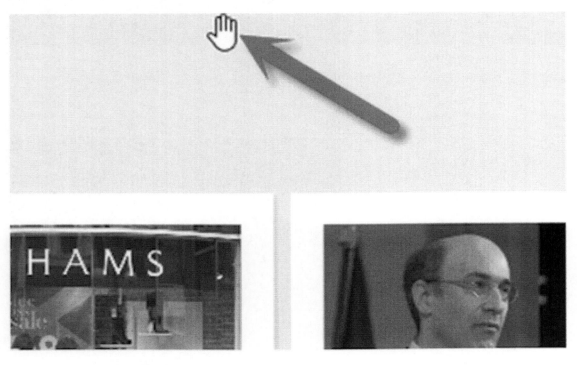

With the hand icon displayed, click the left mouse button and hold it down.

Drag the hand to the bottom of your screen.   As you start to drag, the window detaches from the top of the screen and floats there:

Keep dragging it downwards until it eventually snaps to the bottom of the screen.

At this point, you can release the mouse button and the app will be closed down.

NOTE: This might sound silly even to mention it, but it has caught me out a few times.   If you are using dual monitors on your computer, with one sitting above the other, then trying to close the app from the top monitor in this way will only move it from the top display to the bottom.

If you are on the desktop and you know you have open apps that need to be closed, you can close them from the desktop.

Move your mouse to the top left "hotspot corner", and then run it vertically down the screen to reveal a list of open Metro apps in the "switch list".

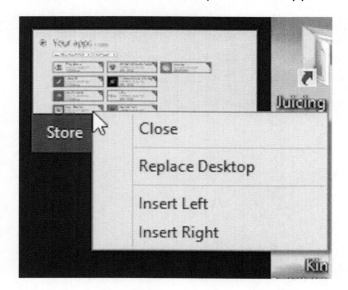

Right click the app you want to close, and select "Close" from the popup menu that appears.   The sidebar remains in place, so you can repeat the procedure for any other apps you might want to shut down.

Searching from the start screen

Press the **Windows Key** to access the start screen.

We are going to look at searching in more detail in the "How To" section of this book, but for now, if you want to search for something from the start screen, just start typing.   As you do, the search feature automatically opens.

For example, if you want to run Microsoft Word, go to the start screen and start typing "Word" (without quotes of course).

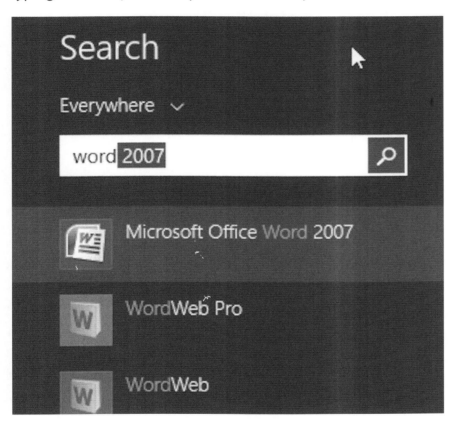

Matches will show up under the search box.

By default, the search feature will look **Everywhere**.

The options you have for searching are found in the drop down menu at the top:

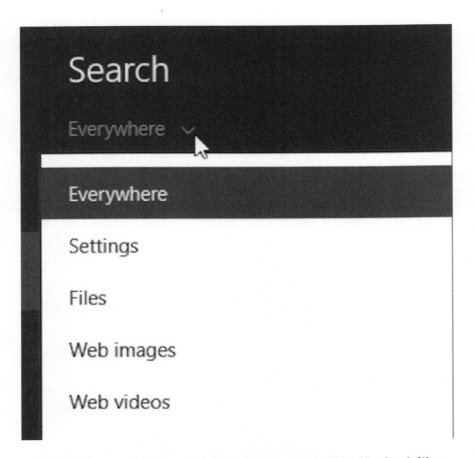

You can change the search settings to specifically find files or even computer settings by clicking on the **Files** or **Settings** icons under the search box.   Other options allow you to find web images or videos.

When you get use to this, I think you'll find it quicker and more efficient than the old Windows Start Menu.

Where is the old start button?

When the Windows 8 desktop shows itself for the first time, things don't look too different from Windows 7.   The Start button is in the bottom left as usual, but it looks different and performs differently.

Clicking it only opens up the Start Screen.   In previous versions of Windows, the Start button would open up a cascading menu system for accessing all of the applications on your computer.   Personally, I prefer the new Windows 8 Start Screen as I find it far more powerful.   However, when you first migrate to Windows 8, learning to live without the features of the old start button means rethinking the way you find and open your apps.

Adding the old start button back

There are a couple of applications (at least) that can do this.   The one I recommend you try is called "Classic Shell" which is free.   It can replace the new Windows Start button with one that is far more familiar.

You can download it here:

http://www.classicshell.net/

Download and install the application and you'll see a start menu appear bottom left.

Here is a screenshot of the start menu on my computer using Classic Shell:

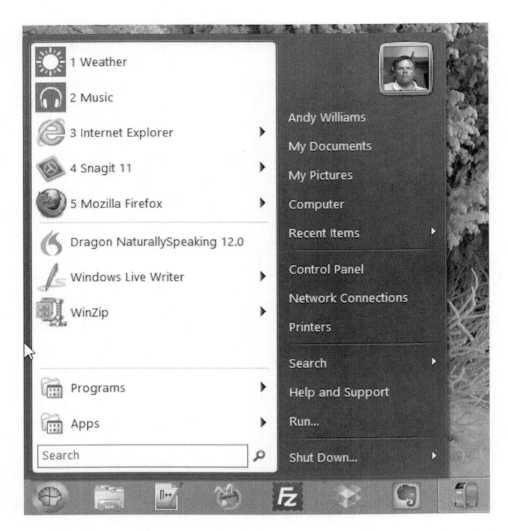

The button itself is the "Shell" icon bottom left, but the rest of the start menu looks very familiar, doesn't it?

If you prefer the start menu from Vista/7 or XP, you can have that too. This application has a wealth of settings and features to play around with but you really should read the help files which come with the application to get the most out of it. I will show you one setting that I use.

If you right-click the start button itself, a menu appears with various options. Now click on **Settings**.

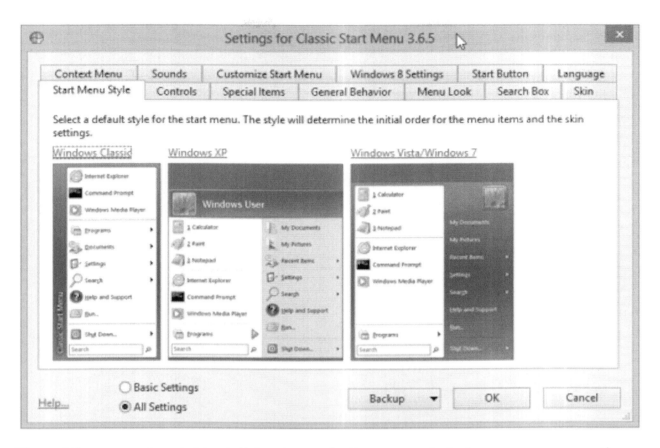

The settings open in a tabbed dialog box.   In the screenshot above, you can see the three styles of start menu available.

On the **Windows 8 Settings** tab (back row, fourth from left), the option I have set is:

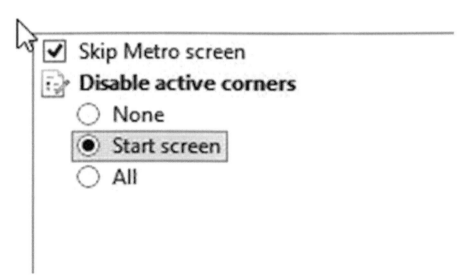

The **Skip Metro screen** is checked.   This means that my Windows 8 machine boots directly to the desktop after login, instead of going to the Metro start screen.

Also, I have the start screen corner (bottom left) disabled so I don't get the Metro icon appearing when I move my mouse to the bottom left.   If you leave this enabled, you'll find that icon appearing a lot when you are trying to open you start menu, which can be a bit bothersome!

The Charms bar

To access the Charms Bar, position your mouse pointer over the hotspot on the top right of the screen and then move it vertically downwards.   Alternatively, position your mouse at the bottom right corner, and then move it vertically up the screen. For those that struggle with this manoeuvre, you can also access the Charms bar by using the keyboard shortcut:

Windows Key + C

When the Charms bar appears on the right, you'll also see the date and time show in the lower left of your screen, along with network and battery indicators.

The Charms bar is a universal toolbar accessible from anywhere in Windows.   It gives you access to basic actions within Windows 8, via 5 icons - Search, Share, Start, Devices and Settings.   We'll look at each of these separately, and I'll also show you some keyboard shortcuts to access each of these sections directly.

Search

Keyboard Shortcut: **Windows Key + Q**

The search button allows you to search for anything on your computer.

This search feature built into Windows 8 is very fast.

When you type into the search box, you'll see results that Windows 8 thinks you are interested in.   The default is to search "everything" on your computer, but as I mentioned previously, if you want to search for a specific item, you can choose to just search for settings or files.

Underneath the list of files on your computer, you'll see a number of search terms:

Clicking on these will open up the Bing Smart Search feature:

Angry Birds Space

Angry Birds Star Wars

2 apps

article-friendly-directories.txt
25/01/2012 21:13
15.7 MB

ELGG_ULTIMATE_sample_plusPR.txt
18/03/2012 18:25
16.1 KB

Pr1+ Blog posts to comment on li...
26/07/2012 09:27
191 KB

how to google 18000.txt
15/11/2013 10:13
490 KB

2013-07-09.csv
22/11/2013 07:57
8.53 KB

2013-07-09.csv
13/12/2013 18:58
8.53 KB

See all 48 documents

Angry Birds Chrome

chrome.angrybirds.com

Play Angry Birds online in HD with Google Chrome.
We're sorry, but it appears that your browser does not
currently support the web technologies needed to play
Angry Birds.

Angry Birds - The O
Angry Birds

angrybirds.com

The Official Home of Angry E
and go shopping

Powered by ᑲ bing

In this screen, you can see the files on my computer on the left. On the right are Bing powered search results, and you can scroll across to the right to see more results.

There is little point in opening the Charms bar, clicking on the search button, and then beginning your search. That requires more mouse work and possibly a keyboard shortcut too. The simplest way to search is to hit the Windows Key and start typing your search query. This is typically what I do instead of going through the Charms bar. It means I have one less keyboard shortcut to remember.

We'll come back to searching later in the "How to" section of the book.

Share

Keyboard Shortcut: **Windows Key + H**

The share button, as the name suggests, is used to share information.

If you are working in a desktop app, you'll be prompted to share a screenshot of the desktop:

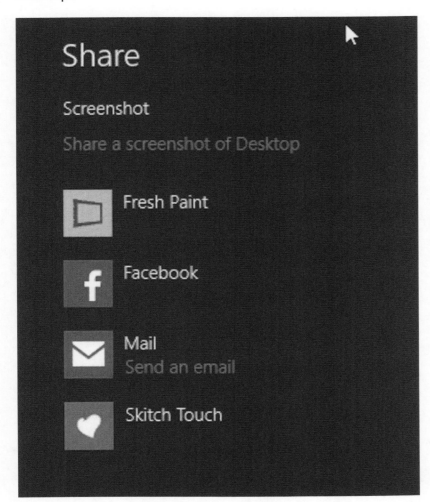

If you are working in a Metro App, you'll have other options.

To see the sharing in action, open or create an image in **Fresh Paint**

Click the Share button (or Windows Key + H) and you'll be given options to share the image.

In the screenshot above, I have options to share my "untitled painting" with Fresh Paint, Facebook, Mail (if I want to email the image to someone), Skitch Touch (a note-taking application) and you may have an option for SkyDrive (which will save the image to your SkyDrive online storage account).

When you click one of the sharing options, a window will open where you'll need to confirm that you want to go ahead and share.

Share to Skitch Touch

Just click the Share to ... button to confirm.

The sharing screen will then close, so as to allow access to the shared item in the app you shared it with.   You then need to open that app.

Besides sharing the "untitled image", I do have other options available for sharing:

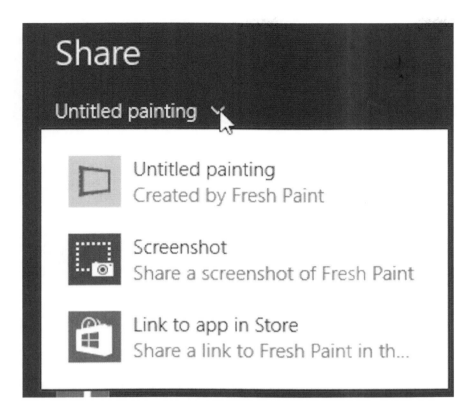

The other options here are a screenshot, or a link to the Fresh Paint App in the app store.

You can go directly to the Share section of the Charms bar with the following Keyboard shortcut:

Windows Key + H

Start

The Start button in the Charms bar takes you to the start screen. I really don't see any need to use this on a non-touch device. I suppose it does make sense for touch screen tablets though.

For normal computer users, simply press the "Windows" key on your bottom left side of your keyboard to access the start screen.

Devices

Keyboard Shortcut: **Windows Key + K**

The Devices screen shows you the various devices that are attached to your computer.

In my devices list, I just have these options:

The last option, project, allows me to extend my computer monitor to a second screen. Clicking that option gives me another menu:

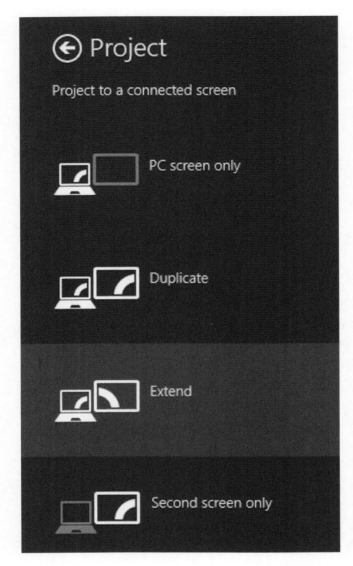

This allows me to define how the second screen will behave. In my case I want it to "extend" my desktop, effectively giving me two desktops to work on.

You can access the Devices setting directly without going to the Charms bar first by pressing the keyboard shortcut:

Windows Key + K

Settings

Keyboard Shortcut: **Windows Key + I**

The Settings button gives you access to all of the settings on your computer.

Click the Settings button to go to the Settings panel.   At the top, you'll see:

From here you can access the Control Panel, the "Personalisation" section of the Control Panel, the "System" section of the Control Panel, and Windows "Help and Support".

At the bottom of the Settings panel you will see:

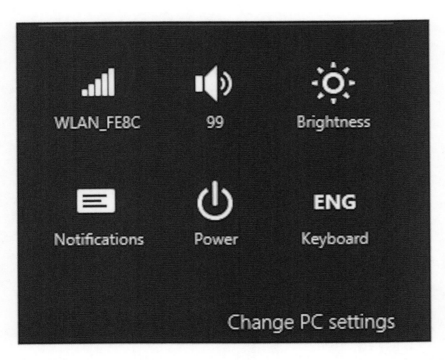

This section gives you various bits of information about your computer. They are: Network connection, sound volume, screen brightness, any notifications you might have, and the keyboard & language settings. You can change these by clicking the appropriate icons. For example, if I want to change my network status to Airplane mode, I can click the network settings, and then flick the Flight mode switch to "On" in the Network panel

Note: Flight mode is a function that turns off all wireless radio parts of a device. This mode is for safe use on aircraft and other places where radio transmitters are prohibited.

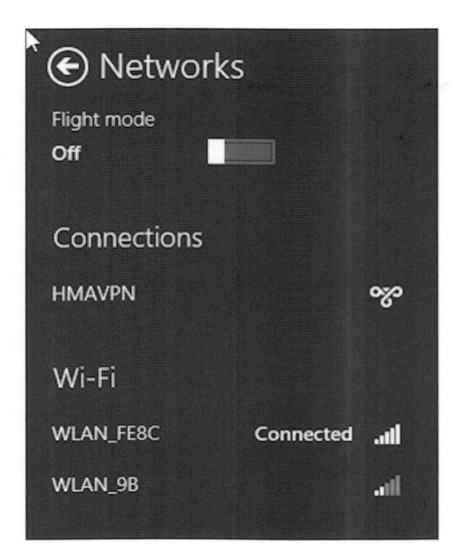

Networks

Flight mode
Off

Connections

HMAVPN

Wi-Fi

WLAN_FE8C   Connected

WLAN_9B

I could of course also switch to a different WIFI on this screen by selecting the one I want to use in the Wi-Fi list.

Another important part of the Setting panel is the Power switch.   This is one way of turning your computer off.

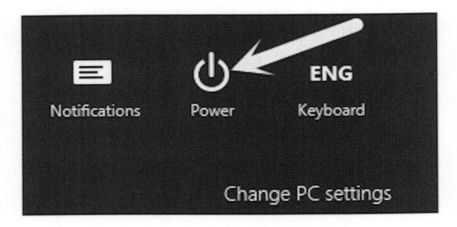

Clicking this button gives you three options in a popup menu:

You can put your computer to sleep, shut it down or restart it.

The Settings bar also has one other very important feature.   The **Change PC Settings** link, bottom right:

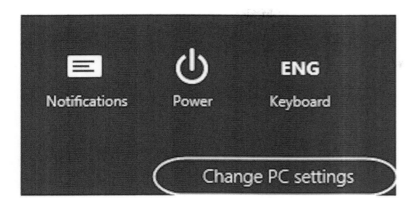

This opens the PC Settings screen:

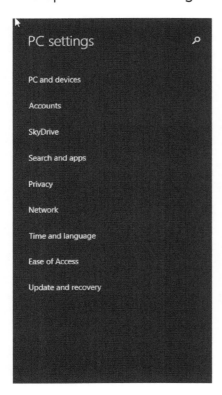

These settings are mostly related to the personalisation of your computer.   We will look at these in the PC Settings section of this book.

You can access the Settings section of the Charms bar directly by pressing the keyboard shortcut:

Windows Key + I

PC settings

The PC Settings screen is accessible from the Settings bar which you can access using the keyboard shortcut:

Windows Key + I

When the settings bar opens, click the link at the very bottom to **Change PC Settings**.

The PC Settings screen looks like this:

On the right, you can get quick access to some of the personal settings like the Lock screen, account picture and picture password. Click the image to access those settings. Alternatively, these three settings are accessible via the **Accounts** menu item on the left.

Let's look briefly at each of the sections on the PC Settings screen.

PC and devices

Clicking on PC and devices opens up a new screen with a number of settings:

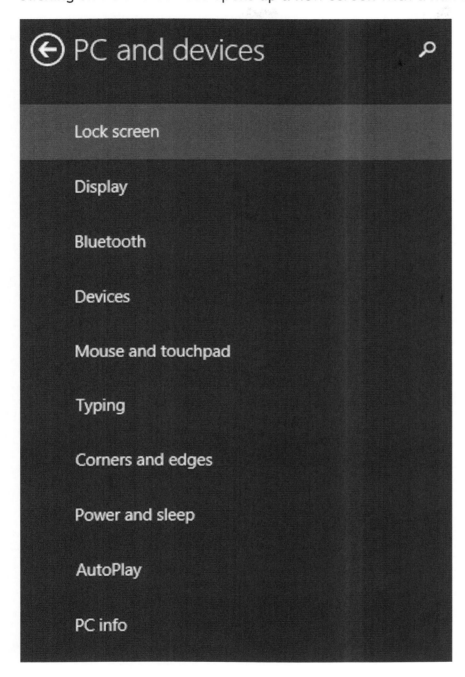

As you select an option on the left, the window on the right changes to offer you access to those settings.

Lock Screen

The Lock screen settings allow you to change the background image to be used by the lock screen, as well as define the lock-screen applications (we saw this earlier in the book).

Display

This option allows you to setup multiple displays. We look at adding a second monitor in the "How To.." section of this book.

Bluetooth

This allows you to switch Bluetooth on or off. You will also be shown the Bluetooth devices attached to your computer, and any others close by that your computer has detected.

Devices

This allows you to view all devices (e.g. printers, monitors, etc) attached to your computer and add new devices

Mouse and touchpad

These options allow you to specify some simple features of your mouse. For example if you are left-handed, you can swap the mouse buttons so the primary button on your mouse is the right one.

You can also control the action of the scroll wheel.

The touchpad options on this screen allow you to specify a delay. This can be useful if you find your touchpad is accidentally triggering when you are typing.

Typing

These options allow you to toggle autocorrect on or off. You can also toggle the highlighting of misspelt words.

Corners and edges

These options define how the corners of your monitor react when the mouse is positioned there. Options include turning app switching on or off, and switching between recent apps with a swipe from the left (which is more useful for touch screen devices). You can also turn off the top right and top left corners from showing the Charms bar and recent apps respectively.

Power and sleep

These are energy saving options.   You can set Windows up to turn your screen off after a specified time if on battery power (or if connected to the power supply).

You can also make your computer go to sleep after a specified interval of inactivity.

Autoplay

Whe you insert a CD, connect a mobile phone or tablet, etc, your computer wants to respond in the most appropriate way.   For a DVD, it might want to automatically play the movie.   For an SD memory card, it might want to connect the card as a new storage device that you can use.   These actions are called "autoplay", and this screen allows you to define how you want autoplay to work with your accessories.   As an example, I have mine set up to open File Explorer when a removable drive or memory card is connected:

PC Info

This screen gives you basic information about your computer, like the processor, RAM installed, system type and Windows version.

That's it for the PC and devices options.   You can go back to the main Settings menu by clicking the small left-pointing arrow next to the PC and Devices menu title:

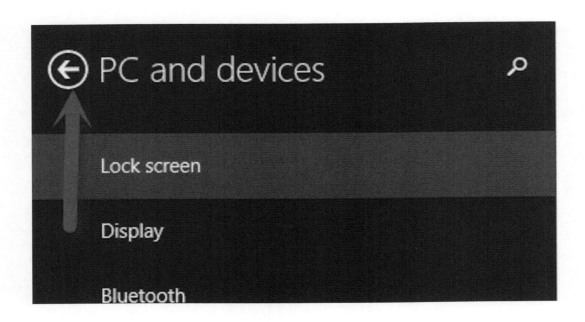

Accounts

The accounts settings screen offers you three items in the menu:

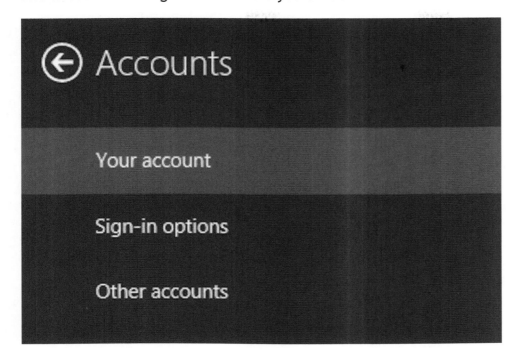

Your Account

The **Your account** settings allow you to change your account photo, or create an account picture. You can also disconnect from your account, and manage more account settings online.

Sign-In Options

This screen allows you to change your password, create a picture password, set or change a PIN to be used for logging in, or removing the request for a password when waking the PC from sleep.

Other Accounts

Want more people to have access to your computer? You can add more accounts here.

SkyDrive

Skydrive is Microsoft's online storage facility for Windows users. The amount of free space you have for Skydrive may depend on when you bought Windows 8, or if you have purchased more space. My installation gives me 7 GB of online storage for free.

The SkyDrive settings menu has four options:

File Storage

These options will show you how much space you have and how much you have used. If you don't use SkyDrive, you should turn off the "Save by default", since otherwise Windows tries to save to Skydrive as a default location.

Camera Roll

Windows wants to automatically upload your photos and videos to SkyDrive. You can disable this feature here.

Sync Settings

If you use multiple Windows 8 devices, you can synchronize all of your devices using SkyDrive.

Syncing is only available if you are signing into your computer with a Microsoft account.

This screen allows you to turn syncing between devices On or Off.   If On, then you can specify exactly what it is you want synced from:

- Personalise settings

- Desktop personalisation

- Password

- Ease of access settings

- Language preferences

- App settings

- Browser settings

- Other Windows settings

You also have the option to turn sync Off when using metered connections (and when "roaming"), to prevent unnecessary charges.

Metered Connections

These options allow you to choose whether or not to upload/download to SkyDrive when you are connected to a metered connection.

Search and apps

The Search and apps settings menu has five items.

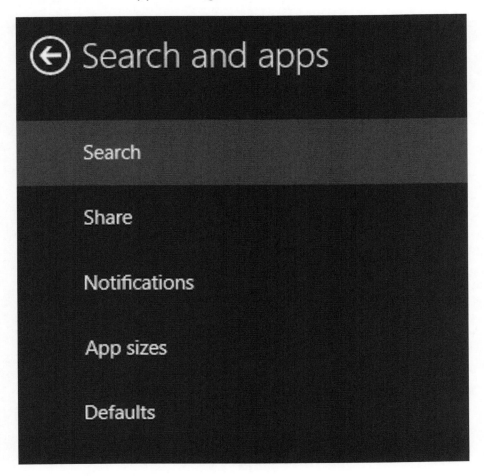

Search

There are a number of options in the search settings.

You can clear your search history.   This will delete all of the data stored about your search behaviour.

By default, when you search from the Start screen, you will get offered search suggestions from Bing search engine (underneath any matches for documents and apps on your computer).   You can switch these off if you do not want them.

You can also choose whether to get personalised results from Bing that use your location, or not.

Safe search is a feature that allows you to hide adult material from the search results. This is very useful if your kids are using your computer.

Also on this screen, you can define how the search works over metered connections or when you are roaming.   If you don't want search results shown under those conditions, you can turn them off.

Share

These options allow you to define which apps you want appearing in the share list, and the order they appear.   Any apps you don't want to share to can be removed, and you can specify whether you want to show the most commonly used apps at the top of the list.

Notifications

Notifications are messages from Metro apps.   This screen allows you to tell Windows how you want to be notified.   For example, it might be that the calendar app needs to tell you about an appointment you have, and if messages from the Calendar app are important to you, you should have them turned on here.   You could also turn notification sounds on or off so you get an audible cue when a message is displayed.

At the top, you have three global settings from where you can turn things On or Off:

Notifications

Show app notifications

On

Show app notifications on the lock screen

On

Play app notification sounds

On

The first option allows you to turn off *all* notifications.

The second option allows you to specify whether you want an app to push notifications onto the lock screen.

The final option is whether or not you want a sound to play when there is a new notification.

Just click these bars to change the setting.

Under these global settings, you can turn notifications On or Off for each Metro app that's active on your computer:

Show notifications from these apps

Angry Birds Space	On	▭▬
Angry Birds Star Wars	On	▭▬
Calendar	On	▭▬
Cut the Rope	On	▭▬
eco Utility	On	▭▬

You will probably want to leave these turned on to begin with, but if any app starts sending you annoying notifications, you can come in here and turn off the notifications for just that particular app.

App sizes

This section of the settings tell you exactly how much space each of the apps on your computer is taking up on your hard disk.   If you are running low on disc space, this screen is useful to help you decide what to get rid of:

App sizes

You have 433 GB of space available on your PC. If you want to uninstall an application, select it from the list, then tap or click Uninstall.

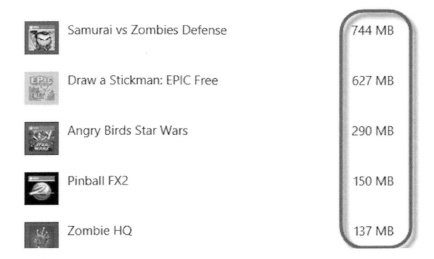

Samurai vs Zombies Defense	744 MB
Draw a Stickman: EPIC Free	627 MB
Angry Birds Star Wars	290 MB
Pinball FX2	150 MB
Zombie HQ	137 MB

Defaults

This is where you can define default apps for specific file types.   You have options for Web browser, email, music, video etc.   You can change the defaults by clicking on the current default application:

Choose default applications

Web browser

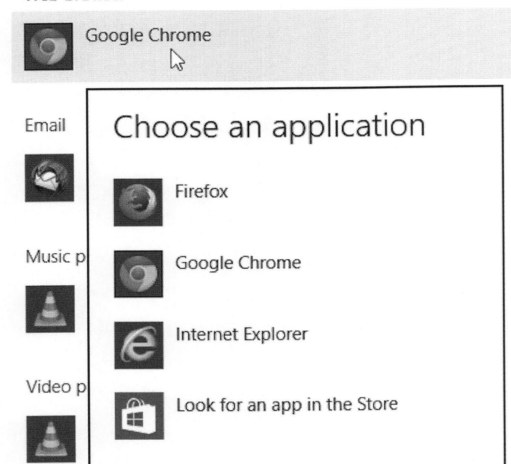

Google Chrome

Choose an application

Email

Firefox

Google Chrome

Music p

Internet Explorer

Video p

Look for an app in the Store

78

Privacy

The privacy menu has several options:

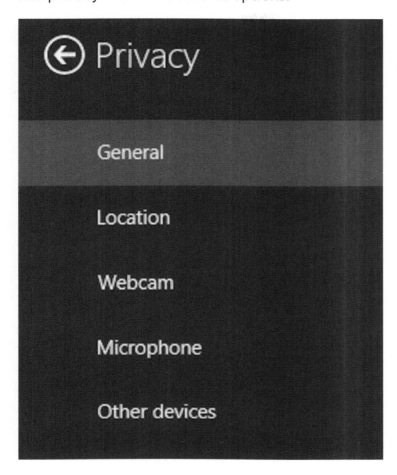

General

There are switches on this screen that allow you to toggle on and off a number of privacy settings.   These are:

Change privacy options

Let applications access my name, picture and other account info

On

Let apps use my advertising ID for experiences across apps (turning this off will reset your ID)

On

Turn on SmartScreen Filter to check web content (URLs) that Windows Store apps use

On

Show text suggestions based on what I type and write on this PC (turning this off will reset suggestions)

On

Let websites provide locally relevant content by accessing my language list

On

Manage my Microsoft advertising and other personalisation info

Privacy statement

So if you don't want applications to have access to your name, picture or account info, you can switch that off here.

Generally, these options allow you to protect your identity as you use your computer.

Location

Do you want your computer to know where you live?   Do you want specific apps serving you content based on where you live?   This screen is where you can configure all of this.   You can turn apps on and off on an app-by-app basis, so you could let "Maps" know your location, but hide it from a news app.

Webcam

Do you want applications to be able to use your webcam?   If not you can turn this off in this screen.   You can do this up on an app-by-app basis, allowing some, but not others.

Microphone

As with the webcam, you can allow or deny various applications use of your microphone.

Other devices

If you have any other devices that applications can access, they will appear on this screen, and you can configure them individually as in the previous screens.

Network

The network options allow you to setup your connections. There are 5 different sections of the network settings:

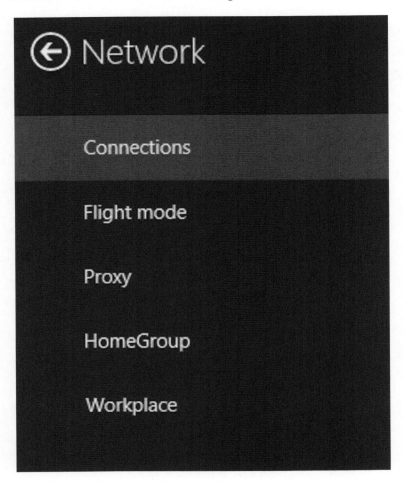

Connections

This screen will show you your currently connected WiFi, Ethernet and VPN status. You can add VPN connections on this screen, as well as edit and remove VPN connections already configured on your system.

Flight Mode

This screen allows you to turn flight mode on or off. Turning flight mode on basically stops all wireless communications, which is useful when you are on a plane.

You also have the ability to turn WiFi & Bluetooth off individually.

Proxy

This area of the settings allows you to manage proxy servers, and to turn one on or off if it's configured.

Homegroup

Homegroups allow you to share files and devices with other people on the network. This screen allows you to set one up. We'll look at how to do that in the "How To" section of the book.

Workplace

If you are part of a workplace network, this is where you configure it. This isn't something most home users will use.

Time and Language

The time and language settings have two sections:

Date and Time

This screen allows you to set your time zone.   You may have other options like "Adjust for daylight savings automatically", though they will depend on your time zone.   You can also change date and time formats.

Region and language

This allows you to specify where you live and what language you want to use in Windows.   In the How To section of the book, we'll see how to add a new language to Windows.   The good news is that you can easily use Windows in one country, while having Windows itself in any language you like.   With previous versions of Windows, this was not always possible without a costly upgrade.

Ease of Access

There are several sections in these options:

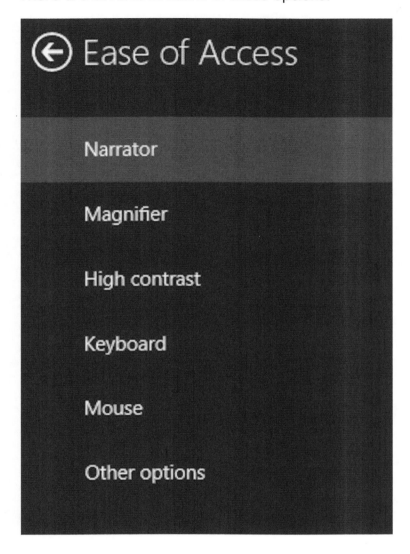

Narrator

You can have Windows read everything to you.   The Narrator can be turned on or off on this screen as well as choose a voice and define what exactly is read to you

Magnifier

The magnifier is essentially an enlargement of the screen.   As you move your mouse around the screen, you can have the magnifier follow your mouse, magnifying anything under the pointer.   You can also use keyboard tracking instead of the mouse cursor.

This screen allows you to setup the magnifier and toggle it on or off.

High Contrast

One some monitors, things may be a little difficult to read.   These settings allow you to choose a high contrast theme that can make things a little clearer.

Keyboard

Windows comes with an on-screen keyboard which can be turned on or off by on this screen.

Mouse

It's possible to change the default pointer size and colour if you need to for better visibility.

Other Options

These are a few visual options, allowing you to turn animations on/off, show/hide the Windows background and decide on how long notifications last for when they appear on your screen.

You can also adjust the thickness of the mouse cursor.

Update and Recovery

There are three options here:

Windows Update

This screen allows you to decide how updates get installed, and you can manually check for new updates (and install them if you wish).

File History

This option allows you to select a backup drive and have all personal documents backed up to that drive.

Recovery

This screen allows you to recover Windows if you have an issue. The options are to **Refresh your PC without affecting your files, Remove everything and reinstall Windows** or **Advanced Start-up.**

Refresh your PC without affecting your files

After using a PC for any length of time, it starts to slow down due to clutter being left during install/uninstalls, fragmentation of registry, and so on. This button will allow you to refresh your PC without losing any of **your data.** However, while many people are really excited by this option, you should be aware of the following:

• The refresh option will reset your PC settings to the default values.

• It will also remove any Windows applications that you've installed from discs or websites (a list of all removed apps will be saved to your desktop).

Remove everything and reinstall Windows

This option basically does a factory reset of your computer, removing everything and reinstalling Windows 8.   **Warning:**   All data on your computer will be lost. If you need to save any files, make sure you back them up to a separate storage device before reinstalling Windows.

Advanced start-up

This option allows you to restart your computer into the Advanced Boot Options menu.   This allows you to do things like:

• Start your computer for another disc, DVD, USB, etc.

• Trouble Shoot problems, repair your computer (system recovery options), Boot into Safe Mode, etc.

File Explorer

Windows 8 File Explorer is a little different to the Windows Explorer that went before it. It is therefore worth covering the basics here so that you can find your way around.

The biggest difference visually is the use of a "ribbon bar", something that has been a common feature in other Microsoft applications for quite some time:

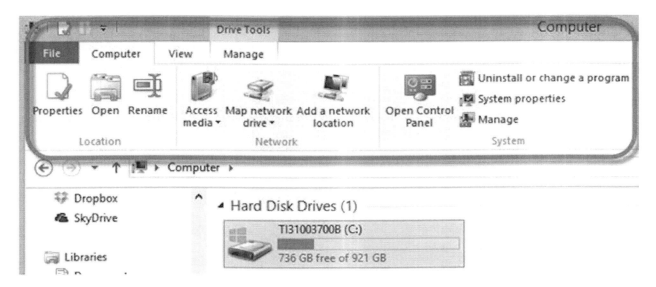

The contents of the ribbon bar change, depending on what is selected below it.

For example, if you have a computer hard disk selected, the "Drive Tools" are opened, giving you access to the actions and features related to disc drive management. In the screenshot above, you can see three tabs in the Drive Tools - Computer, View and Manage.

The **Computer tab** has options related to network devices and also a link to the Control Panel.

The **View tab**, which you will also see when browsing files and folders, allows you to change the way File Explorer displays information. For example, you can choose to show the data as extra large icons, list, small icons, details, etc. You can also choose to hide file extensions and hidden files, etc.

The **Manage tab** allows you to optimize, clean up, or format the selected drive. If it's a DVD or CD drive, you can eject the disc from this ribbon.

The important thing to remember about the ribbon bar in File Explorer is that it is context sensitive. While the Manage tab shows the optimise, clean-up and format options when a drive is selected, it will show Slide Show, and graphics features (like rotate left and right) when images are being explored. Also, when viewing images or documents, other tabs may appear or disappear in the ribbon bar.

Ribbon bar tabs are organised into groups. For example, look at this screenshot of the ribbon bar when I am browsing my "Pictures Library".

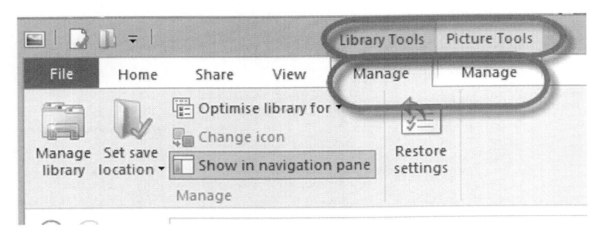

See how there are two groups of tabs - **Library Tools** and **Picture tools**? That's because both of these groups are relevant to the pictures library.

When there are two or more groups showing, the tabs within those groups merge into the ribbon bar. You can see this merger in the screenshot above because both groups contain a tab called Manage, and we end up with two different Manage tabs, one originating from the Library Tools, the other from Picture Tools.

As for the content of the two different manage tabs, you can see the Manage tab from the Library Tools group in the screenshot above. Obviously these "manage tasks" are related to the libraries.

Here is the Manage tab from the Picture Tools group:

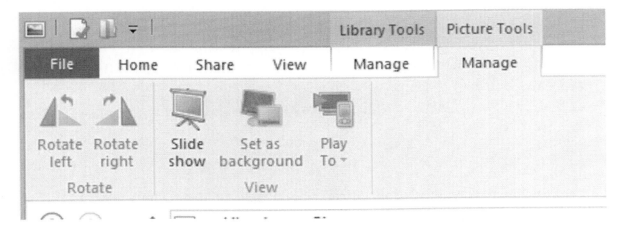

These "manage tasks" are specifically related to pictures.

Another tab you will find in the ribbon bar is the Share tab. It allows you to share files, documents, photos, etc via email, fax, and print, or to members of the Homegroup. You can also burn files to disc from this tab.

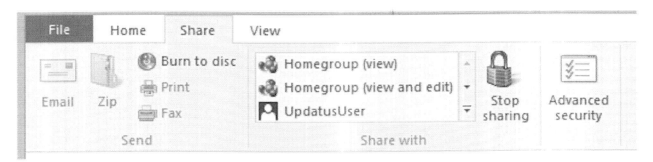

Other tabs include one for Network settings and another for Homegroup settings.

I have never been a fan of ribbon bars in Microsoft applications and Windows 8 File Explorer is no exception. When you first start using a ribbon bar application, it takes some time to find everything, and often longer to achieve the same thing than a simple menu system.

Ultimately, I cannot show you everything in the new File Explorer; you'll need to explore it yourself. Just keep one eye on the Group Name and tabs as you click on various items within the File Explorer. Whatever it is you want to do, it will be there - somewhere!

TIP: Windows 8 File Explorer also makes good use of context sensitive menus. Right click items in the File Explorer to see what options are available to you. You can also right click on the background (where files are displayed) for folder/file settings, like View as:

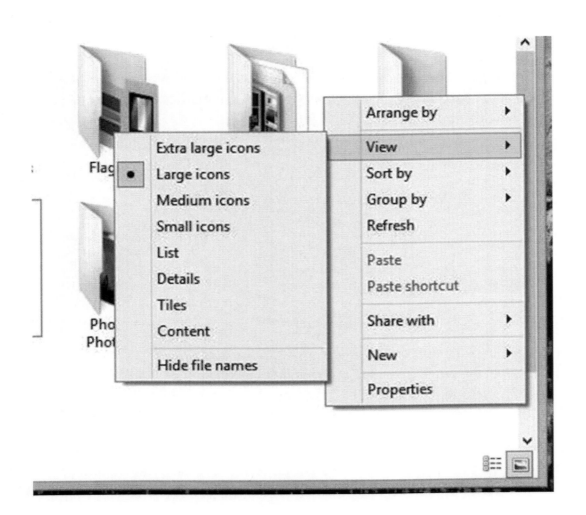

Sky Drive

There are a lot of cloud storage options out there. I personally use Dropbox, but Microsoft do offer 7 gigabytes (GB), of free storage to new Windows 8 users on their cloud service called Sky Drive. However, you will need to have a Microsoft account to get your free cloud storage.

Windows 8 comes with a Metro app for SkyDrive which is accessible from the start screen.

The Metro Sky Drive app is not very intuitive, so I recommend you download the Desktop application and use that instead. This will also allow you to upload larger files (the Metro app and Sky Drive website have 300MB limits).

You can get this from:

https://skydrive.live.com/

Once you install the desktop application, you'll find Sky Drive incorporated into Windows File Explorer.

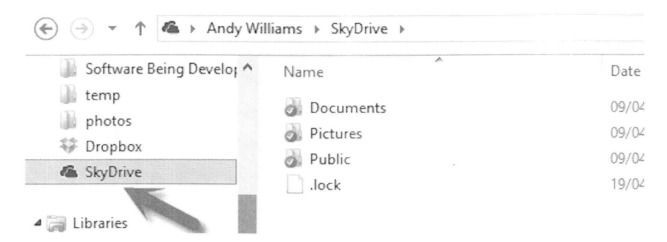

This makes a lot more sense for veteran Windows users.

Anything added to your SkyDrive folder in File Explorer will automatically be synced to your Sky Drive space in the cloud.

If you have multiple devices sharing a Sky Drive account (e.g. phone, tablet & computer), you can access and share your documents between those devices.

WARNING: I have heard of people having their Microsoft Account closed for uploading images that Microsoft felt broke their code of conduct rules. All content you upload to your Sky Drive must obey these rules which you can read here:

http://windows.microsoft.com/en-us/windows-live/code-of-conduct

Since accounts are monitored for violations, the Sky Drive can hardly be seen as secure storage.

How to ...

This section of the book answers a lot of common questions that get asked by people making the switch to Windows 8.

Accessing the Windows 8 control panel

The first way you can access the Control Panel is to go to the start screen and start typing "control panel". Windows 8 will display matches as small tiles on the left of the screen. Click the Control Panel tile to access it.

A second way to access the Control Panel is to open the Setting section of the Charms bar using the keyboard shortcut:

Windows Key + I

The Control Panel link is displayed near the top of the list.

A third way to access the Control Panel is to right-click in the lower left area of the screen (remember that hotspot?), and select Control Panel from the popup menu that appears.

Programs and Features

Mobility Centre

Power Options

Event Viewer

System

Device Manager

Disk Management

Computer Management

Command Prompt

Command Prompt (Admin)

Task Manager

Control Panel

File Explorer

Search

Run

Desktop

Windows Update Settings

Windows Update can be set up to check and install updates at pre-defined intervals. This screen also allows you to do a manual check for updates.

If you want to change the settings for Windows Updates (like the frequency), then you need to go into the Control Panel.

To do this, press the **Windows Key** and start typing "control panel".   When you see it in the search results, click it to open.

In the Control Panel search box, type "update":

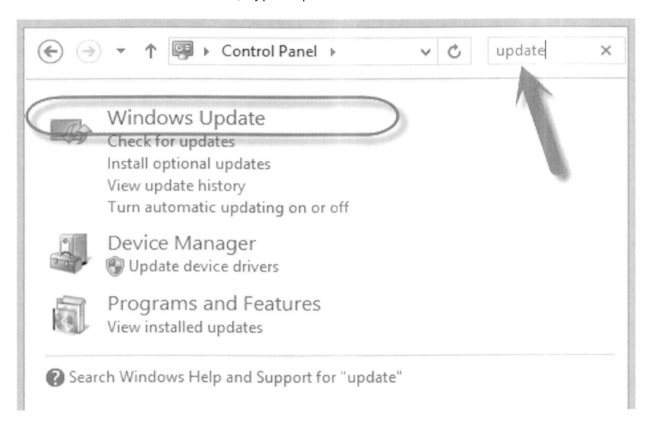

Click on the **Windows Update** link at the top.

You can then select **Change settings** from the menu on the left side:

Control Panel Home

Check for updates
Change settings
View update history
Restore hidden updates

Windows Update

You're set to automatically install updates

1 optional update is
available

Most recent check for updates: Today at 10:33
Updates were installed: 11/04/2013 at 15:00.
You receive updates: For Windows and other products from
                                 Microsoft Update

This will open the Windows Update settings screen where you can choose the frequency of Important Updates.

How to set up a Homegroup

Homegroups allow users within a household to share documents, photos, music, movies, printers, etc, with everyone in the network. Windows 7 and Windows 8 users can join a Homegroup - unfortunately they do not work with Vista or XP.

To set up a new Homegroup use the keyboard shortcut:

Windows Key + I

Click **Change PC Settings.**

Click on Network settings, and then select Homegroup from the options.

If a Homegroup has not already been set up, you'll see an invitation to create one.

HomeGroup

Create a homegroup

With a homegroup you can share libraries and devic
You can also stream media to devices.

Your homegroup is protected with a password and y
share.

NOTE: If you don't see this, and instead you see a series of libraries and devices with switches, then a Homegroup is already set up and ready to use.

When you click the Create button, you'll be asked what you want to share. The options will include documents, music, pictures, videos etc. Your Homegroup is now set up and *almost* ready to go. You will see that a password has been assigned to the Homegroup. You now need to give other computers/users the password so that they can join your new home network.

Sharing in a Homegroup

If you have several devices set up as a Homegroup, it means you can share resources (folders, printers, music, videos, etc), between the devices in that Homegroup. The Homegroup will show up in Windows File Explorer:

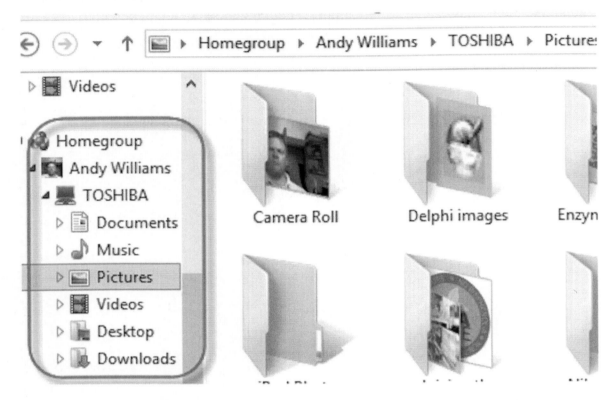

This settings page allows you to define what can be shared from your computer.

Options are:

• Documents

• Music

• Pictures

• Videos

• Printers and Devices

You can allow all devices on the network to share the content if you want (that includes Smart TVs).

To grant membership to the Homegroup, this page also displays the password they need to enter. If you want to change the Homegroup password, you need to do that from the Control Panel.

To go there, press the **Windows Key** and start typing "control panel".

When you see it appear in the search results, just click it to open.

In the Control Panel search box (top right), type "home" and the Homegroup options should be displayed in the window.

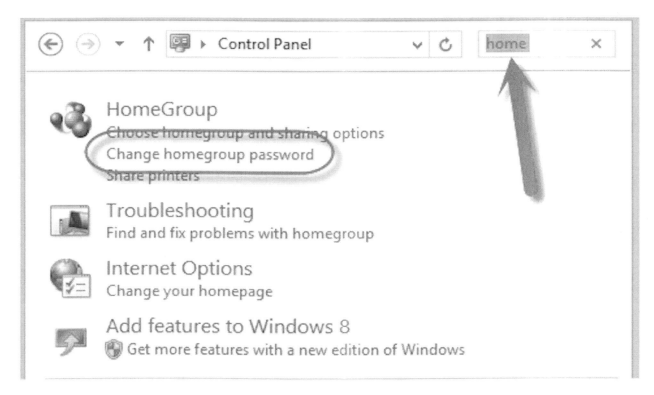

Click the link to **Change Homegroup password**.

The final option on this screen allows you to leave the Homegroup. This just disconnects your computer from the Homegroup network.

Scroll through open apps

In previous versions of Windows, you could scroll through open applications using:

ALT + Tab

This combination still works, and is my preferred method of looking for an open application. **ALT + tab** will show you *all* open applications, whether traditional Windows applications or Metro apps.

There is also a specific way of scrolling through just the open Metro apps. That key combination is:

Windows Key + Tab

This opens the **App switching panel** on the left of the screen:

NOTE: When you release the keys, the app switcher disappears. This key combination is only there so you can switch between open apps. If you want to close a Metro app, the best way is to bring up the App switcher panel using the mouse gesture (mouse top left, then vertically down the screen). You can then right-click and close open apps.

If you are currently using a Metro app when you press the Windows key + Tab combination, the top item in the App switcher will be the desktop (see image above).

If you are using a desktop app when you bring up the App switcher, this desktop item will be missing.

Keeping your finger on the Windows Key, while repeatedly pressing the tab key, you can scroll through the items in this list. To switch to one of the open apps, just release the keys once it's highlighted.

Add a Windows user

If you need to add another user to your computer, press the keyboard shortcut:

Windows Key + I

At the bottom of the right panel, select **Change PC settings.**

The PC settings screen opens.   Now select **Accounts.**

Select **Other Accounts** from the menu.

On the right, click the **Add an account** button.

You will be asked for an email address that the user will use to sign in.   If they have a Microsoft account, use that one.   You then click the **Next** button at the bottom of the screen.   You will then be asked if it is a child's account so that Windows will turn on "Family Safety".

On the same screen, you can click a link bottom left of the screen if you want to "Add a child's account" directly instead of going the above route.

If the user you want to add does not have a Microsoft Account, and doesn't want one, there is a link at the bottom of the screen to create this type of account.   Just follow the instructions in that case.

Note about account types

With Windows 8, there are two types of user account - a Microsoft Account (previously called Windows Live), and a local account.

Microsoft account or local account?

Using a Microsoft account means you sign into your PC with your Microsoft account email address.   This allows you to:

• Download and buy apps from the app store.

• Get online content into Microsoft apps automatically.

• Sync settings (account picture, personalised settings, etc) between multiple Windows 8 devices such as a laptop and tablet.

If you intend to use the Metro apps on Windows 8, you really need to have a Microsoft account.   If you only want to use the Desktop, then you can happily live with a local account.

NOTE: A Microsoft account is required if you want to use apps like Mail, Calendar, People, Messaging & SkyDrive.

Essentially, most people will probably want to sign into Windows 8 with a Microsoft Account, at least initially while they get used to it and decide whether they want access to these additional "Microsoft Account" features.

When you add a new user to your computer, you will need to choose whether to set them up with a Microsoft account or Local account.   You can change it later though, so don't worry too much if you are unsure which option to choose.

Delete a Windows user

In Windows 8 there are a couple of ways we can delete a user.

First way is to go into the same settings we used to set up the account.

Press the keyboard shortcut:

Windows Key + I

At the bottom of the right panel, select **Change PC settings**.

The PC settings screen opens.   Now select **Accounts**.

Select **Other Accounts** from the menu.

Click on the account you want to delete.   You will then get a menu to edit or remove the account.

Another way of deleting a user is to go into the Control Panel.

Press the keyboard shortcut:

Windows Key + I

Select **Control Panel** from the menu on the right.

Depending on how you have your Control Panel set up, you might see the User Accounts section so can click on it.   A quick way to find it if you don't immediately see it is to type "user" into the Control Panel search box.

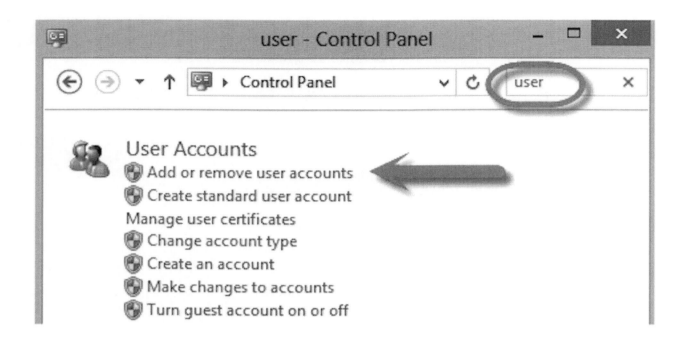

You can now see the User Accounts section where there is a link to Add or remove user accounts.   Click on it.

You will now see a list of users.   Click the one you want to delete.

You can now click the **Delete the account** link in the left hand menu.

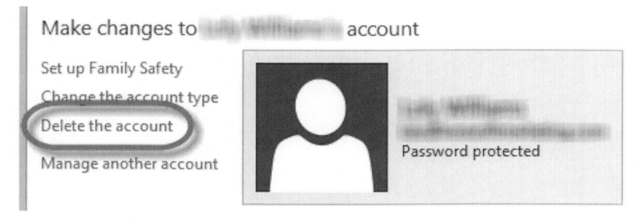

Before the account is deleted, you will be asked whether you want to delete or keep the files associated with that user

There will then be a final confirmation box.   Click the **Delete Account** button to complete the process.

Printing in Windows 8

Printing from traditional Windows applications

Traditional Windows applications typically have a File menu with a print option if applicable.   The typical way to print a document is to open the file in its native application and select Print from the File menu.

Printing from Windows File Explorer

You can print a file directly from File Explorer.

Right click the file you want to print, and select Print from the menu.

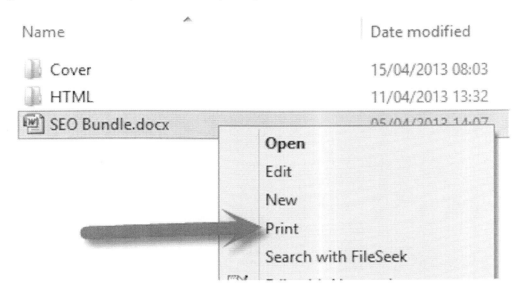

Printing from Metro apps

This is where things are a little less intuitive.

Open the document in its native Metro app.

Open the Devices option from the Charms bar.   You can do this with the keyboard shortcut:

Windows Key + K

You should see your printer listed. If you don't, then you probably haven't installed it, or it is not connected and turned on.

Click on your printer, and you'll be given some printing options (like print quality, number of copies, etc) and a **Print** button to click when you are ready.

Take a screenshot

If you just want to take a screenshot of the entire screen, then you can hold the **Windows Key** down and click the **PrintScreen** (PrtSc) button.

This will save a screenshot of your desktop in the Pictures folder inside a sub-folder aptly named Screenshots.

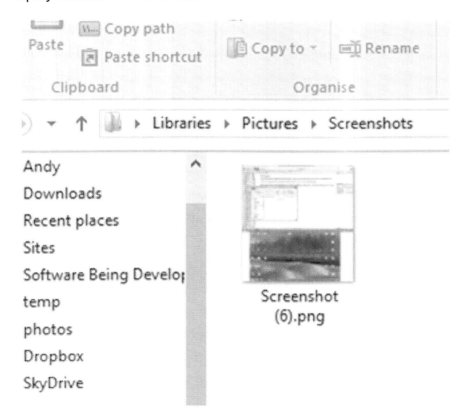

NOTE: on some computers, the PrintScreen button is accessed by holding down a Function key, so that would mean Windows Key + Function Key + PrintScreen.

Also note that if you are using dual monitors, both monitors will be captured and displayed in a single image file.

The Window "Snipping Tool"

If you just want to take a screenshot of a smaller area on your screen, you can use a tool that comes with Windows 8.   It's called the Snipping Tool.   To locate the Snipping Tool, open the start screen and type "snip" to find it.   Run it by clicking on the tile.

Next click the down arrow on the **New** button.

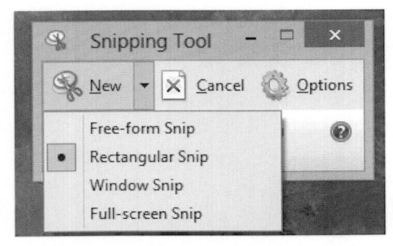

You can select what you want to capture.

• **Free-form snip** allows you to draw freely on your screen with a pen to select the area.

• **Rectangular snip** allows you to draw a rectangle around the area to be captured.

• **Windows snip** allows you to select a Window to capture.

• **Full-screen snip** allows you to capture the full screen.

When you select one of the first three options, the snipping tool is immediately ready for you to define what it is you want to capture.   You'll see that the mouse cursor has changed.   Select the area to capture, and snipping tool will show it to you in a simple editor:

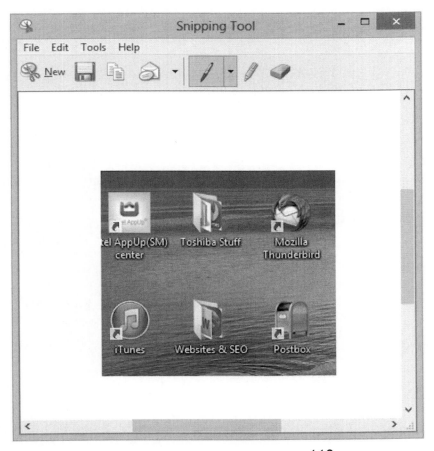

You can annotate your snips with the pen & highlighter tool.   Once happy, you can save your screenshots from the File menu, and then create another snip if you need to.

NOTE: Unlike the first three options, if you select **Full-screen snip**, the screenshot is taken immediately after you select that option.   You don't have to define an area because this option captures the full screen (or full screens if you use multiple monitors).

Create a slideshow of your photos

There are a few ways you can do this.

The first is to use the built in Metro Photos app.

Launch it from the start screen tile. It should be in the first group of tiles, but if you cannot find it, just start typing "photos" and Windows search will find it for you.

You'll see the pictures library, and any other image locations, as tiles at the bottom of the Photos app. Navigate to the folder that you want to use for the slide show (you navigate the folders by clicking the tiles that represent the locations).

When you have found the folder with your slideshow photos, right-click the screen (or use the keyboard shortcut: **Windows Key + Z**), to bring up the command bar at the bottom.

Click the Slideshow button.

The slideshow will now play.

NOTE: If you want to limit your slideshow to just a few photos within a folder, first right-click each image you want to include. This will place a checkmark in the top right of the photo. Now only those images with checks will appear in the show after you click the Slide show button.

Slideshow from File Explorer

Navigate to the folder where your images are located.

You can choose the photos you want to include in the slideshow by selecting them (hold the CTRL key, and then click all of the photos one by one to select them).

Once you have the photos selected, select the **Manage** tab from the **Picture Tools**.

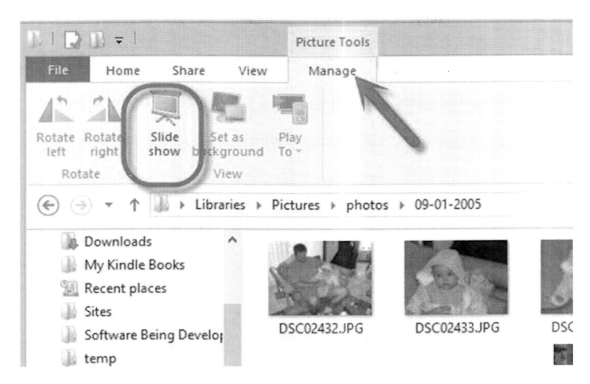

Click the **Slide Show** button.

When this slide show is running, you can right-click anywhere on the screen and choose a few options:

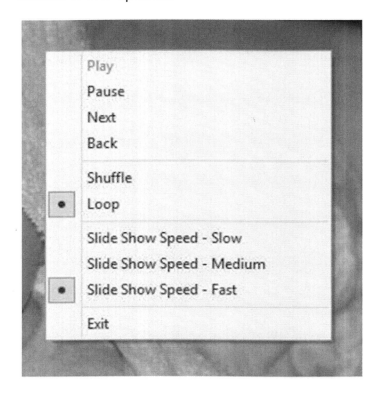

113

TIP: For greater control over your slide shows, and management of your photo library, I recommend you download and install Picasa from Google.   It's free and it is a very powerful organizer, editor and photo sharing tool.

http://picasa.google.com/

Searching in Windows 8

There are a few different ways you can search on your computer, and a few different ways to access the search feature.

The Charms bar (**Windows Key + C**) has a search button which you can click to start the search.   We saw this earlier in the book.

I find it easier to press the **Windows Key** (to access the start screen) and just start typing.   The search screen comes up automatically when you do this.

Whether you access the search feature through the Charms bar or the Windows Key, the default search mode is to **Search Everywhere**.   You can manually switch to **File search** or **Settings search**, but that requires an additional mouse click.

If you know what it is you are looking for, you can use keyboard shortcuts to access each of these three search modes.

Search Shortcuts

Windows Key + Q   Search Everywhere

Windows Key + F   Search Files

Windows Key + W   Search Computer Settings

These keyboard shortcuts help to find the things you want faster.

Manually switching search mode

You can change the type of search by clicking on the options available:

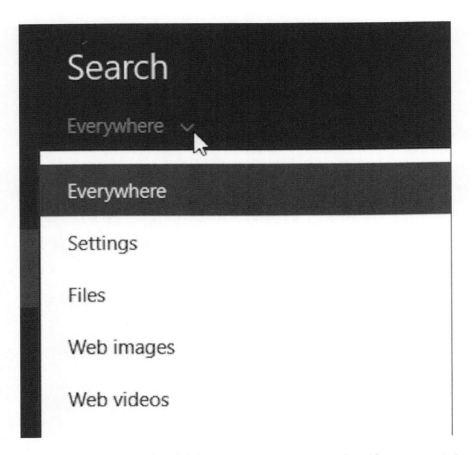

You can also search within apps. For example, if you want to search for weather in Kansas City, click on the Weather App and type "Kansas". I have the Sky News App on my computer, and I can search the news in a similar way.

As you can see, the search features built into Windows 8 are really very powerful.

Windows File Explorer also has a lot of advanced features to help you search.

Advanced searches in Windows 8's File Explorer

When searching for things in File Explorer, you can use a number of advanced features.

The search box is found in the top right corner:

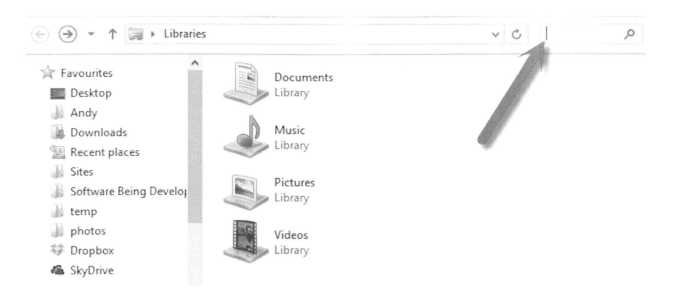

Using Search Tools in Explorer

When you click inside the search box in File Explorer, the **Search Tools** group appears in the ribbon bar.

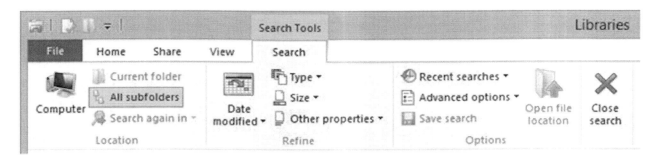

These tools allow you to create advanced searches based on a number of different parameters. For example, clicking on the **Type** drop-down box allows you to search for specific types of documents:

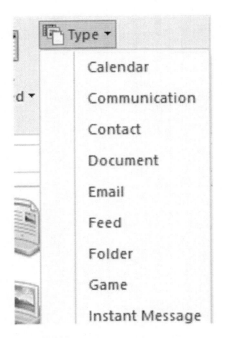

.. and I've only shown you a few of the different options in the type menu. Clicking on an item modifies the search box. If I want to find a folder on my computer, I can click **Folder**, and this is what the search box changes to:

If I click the word "folder" inside the search box, I get the full list to choose from again to modify my search.

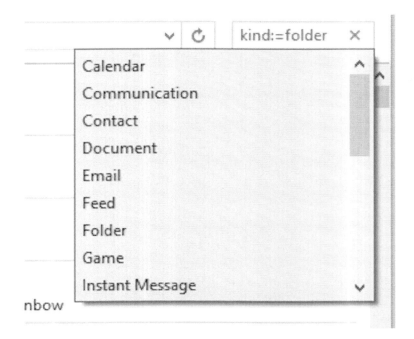

I can also type into the search box to add more information to my search:

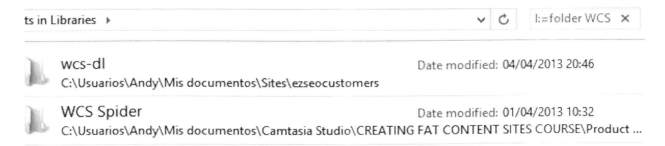

Here I've added WCS to my search for a folder, and Windows finds two folders containing the letters WCS.

Besides document "type", the Search Tools allow you to search by date modified and file size. There are also some other useful search options you can explore while you have the Search Tools open.

Search by file extension

There are search commands not included in the ribbon bar which you might like to use. These include searching for a file by its file extension. This is done with the command Ext: followed by the file extension.

For example, **Ext:.pdf** would search for PDF files. I could modify that further. For example, if I was trying to find a PDF file that had the word affiliate in the filename, I could search with:

Ext:.pdf affiliate

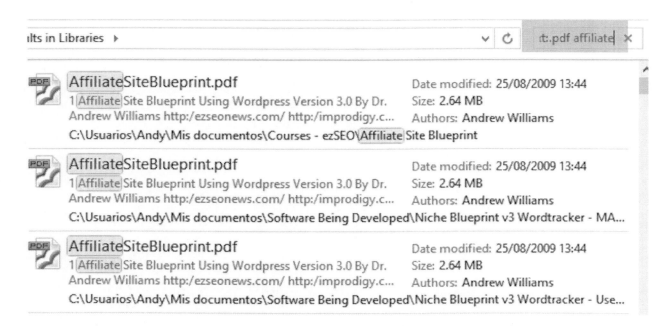

See the search command in the search box top right?

Another useful set of tools that you can type directly into the search box are what's known as Boolean operators.

Using Boolean operators to search

Boolean operators are usually the domain of programmers, but you can use them in your searches as well. They are **AND, OR & NOT** and need to be typed in uppercase. You can actually use the "-" symbol instead of the word NOT as well, which makes things a bit easier.

AND will make sure that matches include both of the words on the right and left of the AND. For example, **car AND nissan** will return results that include both of the words, nissan and car.

OR will make sure that matches include either/or both of the words on the left and right of OR. So **car OR nissan** will return matches for "car" OR "nissan", or both "car" and "nissan".

NOT is my favourite Boolean operator. It allows you to remove options from the search. So, if you search for **car NOT nissan**, then you are searching for items that match the word car, but do not contain nissan. You could also write this as **car - nissan**.

Snapping apps and applications to the sidebar

Windows 8 allows you to snap an app to the sidebar.

Let's look at Metro apps first.

Snapping Metro apps

If you have several open, move your mouse to the top left of the screen, then vertically down to show to app switcher:

Now move your mouse over the app you want to snap to the sidebar, then click and HOLD the left mouse button. Drag the app over to the right sidebar without releasing the mouse button.   As your mouse approaches the right edge of the screen, the right sidebar will slide out.

When it does slide out, drop the app into it by releasing the mouse button.

There is a narrow dividing bar between the app and the rest of your desktop.   In the middle of this divider are three small circles.

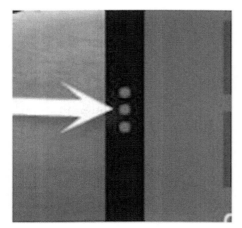

This divider can be dragged to the right or left to resize the width of the snapped app.

As you resize the app smaller, the app will disappear as it is unsnapped from the sidebar.

If you resize it to the full width of your screen, the app takes over the full screen.

You can grab the top of a snapped app with your mouse (move your mouse to the top of that window until the hand cursor appears, then click and hold to grab the window).   Now you can move the snapped window to the other side.

You can even snap two apps on the same screen; one to the left and one to the right.

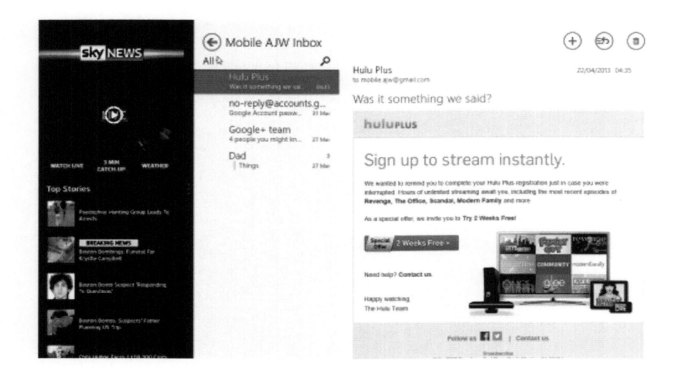

Something to try:

Snap an App to the left side of the screen and then press the keyboard shortcut:

Windows Key + .

Keeping your finger on the Windows key, repeatedly press the ".."

Try the same thing with the **Windows Key + SHIFT + .**

Snapping desktop applications

You can snap desktop applications to the right and left of the screen as well.

Grab the title bar of the application by clicking and holding the mouse button down. Now drag the mouse as far left or as far right as you can.   A bounding rectangle will appear, showing where the application will snap to after you release the mouse button.

Repeat for another application on the other sidebar.

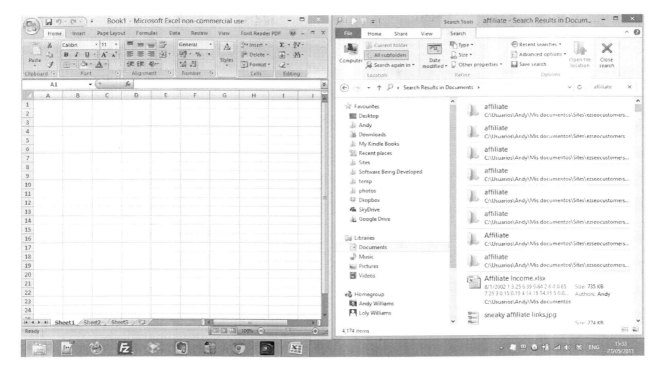

You don't have the central divider that can be dragged like the Metro apps, but it is still very useful to get two apps side by side on your monitor.   To unsnap these apps, just click and hold down the title bar again and then pull it away from the top of the screen.

How to open two copies of File Explorer

Sometimes it is very useful to open two or more copies of File Explorer at the same time, so you can copy files from one location to another, or browse several locations at the same time.

The thing is, if you have File Explorer open, then clicking on the icon in the Taskbar just brings that copy of Explorer to the front.   Not what we want.

To open a second copy of the program from the Taskbar, simply hold the SHIFT key down as you click on the File Explorer icon.

A second copy with open.

How to turn Airplane/Flight mode On/Off

If you are on a plane, or somewhere else where you need to turn off *all* wireless activity, you can put your computer into Airplane/Flight mode.

There are a few ways to do this. The quickest is to click on the Network icon in your taskbar:

The network bar then opens on the right:

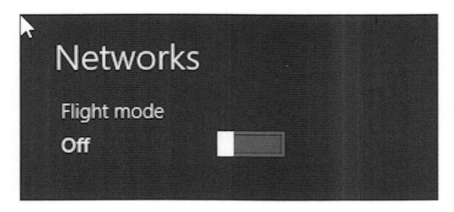

Just click the switch to turn flight mode On.

Another way to do this is by pressing the keyboard shortcut:

Windows Key + I

Then in the sidebar, select the network icon:

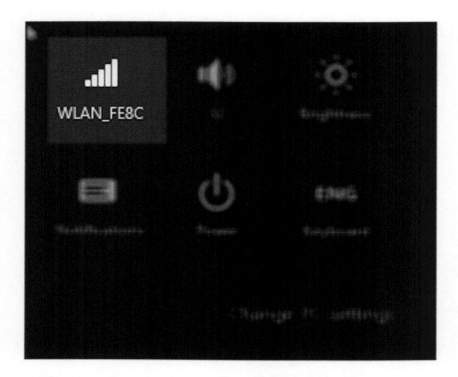

NOTE: Your own network name will be different to mine.

Click it to open the same Network settings bar and then switch Flight mode On or Off as required.

How to open the Windows Task Manager

The Windows Task Manager can be opened in a few different ways.

The keyboard shortcut for this is:

CTRL + SHIFT + Escape

An alternative is to right-click the lower left hotspot and select Task Manager from the popup menu.

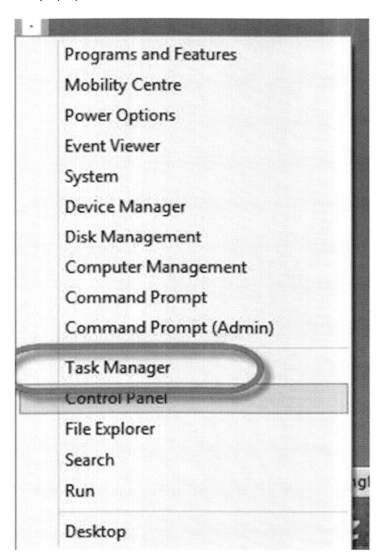

How to shut down, restart or put your computer to sleep

A task as basic as closing down your computer is something that should be obvious, but it's not.

There are several ways to access the close down options.

Firstly, right clicking the Start Button in the bottom left of your screen will open a menu with the option of **Shut down or sign out**.   This is actually a menu that opens out when you move your mouse over it to give you more options:

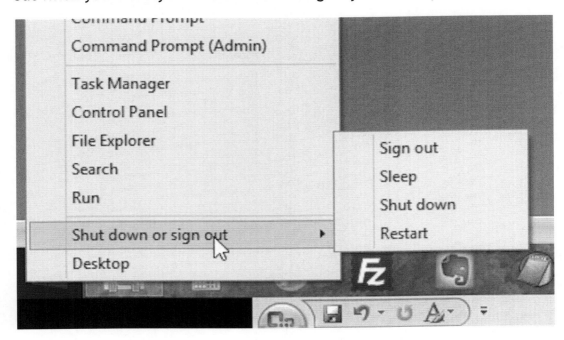

From there you can sign out, put the computer to sleep, shut the computer down or restart the computer.

Another simple way to close your computer down is to press the keyboard shortcut:

Windows Key + I

This brings up the Settings screen.

At the bottom of this screen is the power button. Clicking it opens a menu with three options; **Sleep**, **Shut down** or **Restart.**

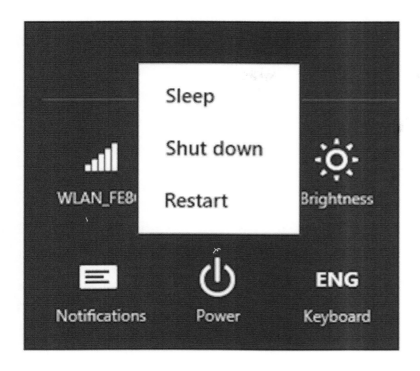

Shut down from the Desktop

Another method is to click on an empty area of the desktop wallpaper (or just click in the Taskbar), and then press the keyboard shortcut:

ALT + F4

This opens the shut down dialog box which allows you to restart, shut down, switch user, sign out, or put the computer to sleep.

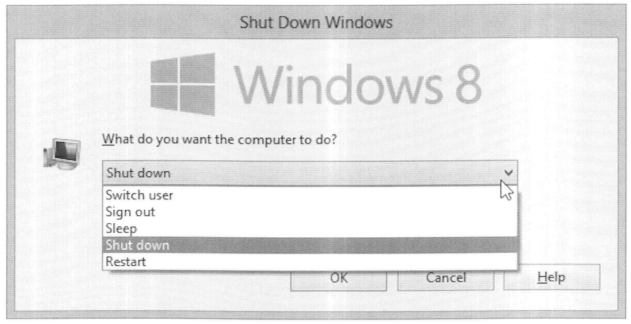

Creating Desktop icons to shut down

If you would like an even quicker way to close down your computer, you can create a shortcut icon on your desktop to do this.

Windows comes with a utility called Shutdown.exe, but it's a command line utility, and not an application you just double click to run. You actually need to pass the utility some parameters to tell it what to do.

We can create desktop icons that run the utility with parameters to shut down, sleep, restart etc.

Right click on a blank bit of desktop and select **New** - **Shortcut**.

In the dialog box that appears, type:

shutdown.exe /s /t 00

Click **Next**, and enter a name for your shortcut (the default will be shutdown.exe since that is the program we are calling with this shortcut). I'll call mine "Close". Click **Finish** to create the shortcut.

The shortcut needs a better looking icon, so right-click it and select Properties:

Now, click the **Change icon...** button:

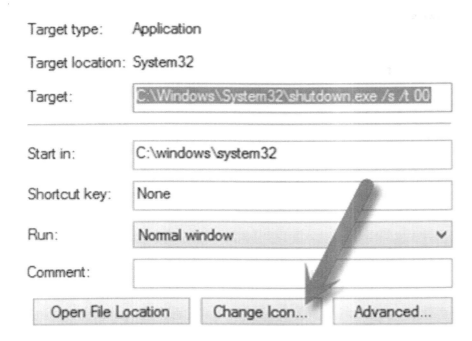

Target type: Application

Target location: System32

Target: [C:\Windows\System32\shutdown.exe /s /t 00]

Start in: C:\windows\system32

Shortcut key: None

Run: Normal window

Comment:

[Open File Location]   [Change Icon...]   [Advanced...]

You'll get a message saying no icon is associated with the shutdown.exe program. That's fine as Windows will open up a set of default icons for you to choose from.

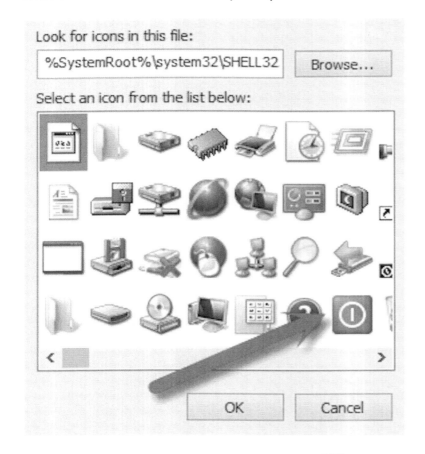

Look for icons in this file:

%SystemRoot%\system32\SHELL32   [Browse...]

Select an icon from the list below:

[OK]   [Cancel]

Select one and click **OK**, and then **OK** again to close the properties dialog.

Your "close down" short cut icon should now appear on the desktop. Double clicking it will close your computer down.

We have just created an icon to close the computer, but you could also create icons for restarting, hibernating and more.

These other icons are created the same way, but have a different set of parameters to pass to the Shutdown.exe utility.

Here they are if you want to try:

Restart: shutdown.exe /r /t 00

Hibernate: rundll32.exe powrprof.dll,SetSuspendState

Manually check for windows updates

We already had a quick look at Windows Updates in the PC Settings chapter, so I'll be brief here.   To check for possible Windows updates press the keyboard shortcut:

Windows Key + I

Select "**Change PC Settings**" at the bottom.

On the PC Settings screen, the bottom item is **Update and recovery**.   Click it.

Windows Update

You're set to automatically install updates

No important updates are scheduled to be installed. We last checked today. We'll continue to check for newer updates daily.

Check for updates now

This will inform you if there are any updates to install.   Windows will check for updates on the schedule defined in the Control Panel.   If you want to change the schedule, see the Windows Update section of the PC Settings chapter.

Mine says there weren't any updates when Windows last checked, but I can manually check for updates by clicking the **Check for updates now** button.   If there are any, you are given the opportunity here to install them.

Change the Desktop wallpaper & create themes

You can change your desktop wallpaper by right-clicking the desktop.

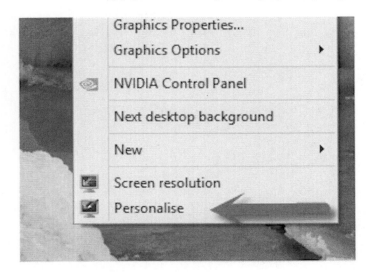

Select **Personalise** from the popup menu.

This brings up the "Personalisation" screen in the Control Panel.   Here you can select a set of pre-installed wallpapers in the "My Themes" area.

At the bottom, the link **Desktop Background** allows you to select your own wallpapers, and set up your own themes.

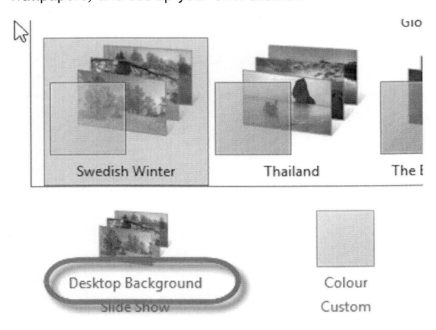

Click the **Desktop Background** link.

136

You can now choose a folder on your computer that holds the image(s) you want to use for your desktop background/theme.

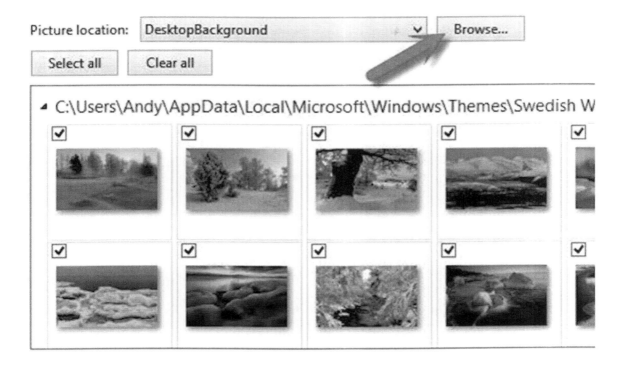

When you select a folder, all images in that folder will be shown in the box below with checks next to each one. Make sure you only check the one(s) you want to use as your background.

TIP: Create a folder in your Pictures library called "backgrounds" and add all of the photos you would like to use as a desktop background to this folder. Then select this folder as the picture location and you'll be able to set up your own theme, using your own photos.

When you have selected the image(s) you want to use, click the **Save changes** button at the bottom. Your theme will be saved as "Custom" in the "My themes" area.

Notice that on this screen, you can also modify the picture "change frequency" and position of the image on the screen:

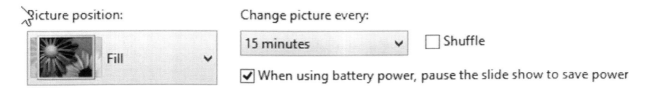

View basic information about your computer

The System screen in the Control Panel gives you basic information about your computer, like operating system version, manufacturer, processor, RAM (installed memory), etc.   It also gives your computer a **Rating** which Microsoft calls the **Windows Experience Index.**   The higher this number, the better Windows will run on your computer.

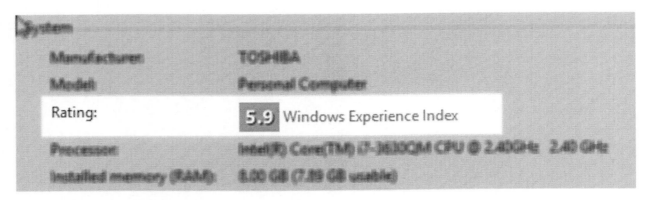

Clicking the "Windows Experience Index" link takes you to a screen that shows you the scores for each major component of your computer.

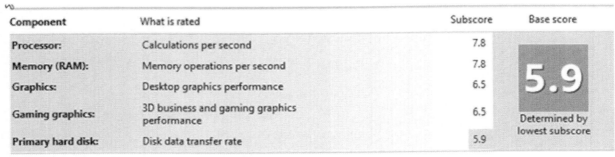

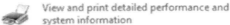
View and print detailed performance and system information

I can see from my score that the hard disk is the main component slowing this computer down.   However, for my needs, it's fine.

TIP: If you ever go to buy a laptop, check this score and compare the laptops you are interested in.   You'll be surprised how much variation there is.

You can get to the System screen in a number of different ways.

The easiest way is to press the keyboard shortcut:

Windows Key + Pause/Break

NOTE: Depending on your computer, you may need to press the Fn key to access the pause/break function.   Therefore it would be Windows Key + Fn + Pause/Break.

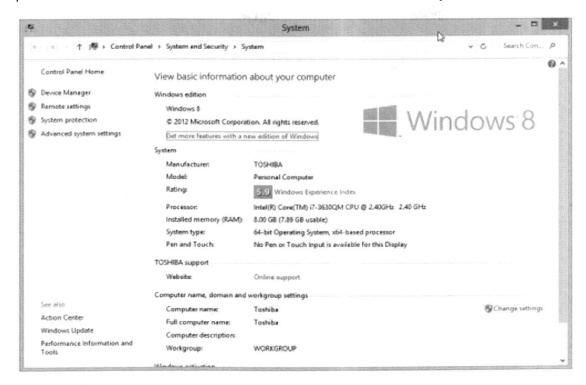

Another way you can get here is from Windows File Explorer.

If you click on Computer in the left panel, you'll see the computer tab in the ribbon bar.   Select properties:

Zooming with CTRL + mouse wheel

This will be dependent on the application you have open, but in many applications you can hold the CTRL key down and use your mouse wheel to zoom in and out.

In a word processor or text editor, this usually changes the font zoom level. You can use this to increase or decrease font size displayed on your monitor. It should be noted that this does not change the actual document's font size, just how it is displayed on the monitor.

If you are working with File Explorer, CTRL + mouse wheel changes the size of the file/folder icons, in much the same way that the options in the View menu does.

If you are on the start screen, CTRL + mouse wheel will change the zoom level of the application tiles.

The other place this shortcut comes in handy is in your web browser. CTRL + mouse wheel can increase/decrease the zoom level of the text and images on the page, making it easier to read.

Changing the time zone

Setting the time zone on your computer can be done by pressing the keyboard shortcut:

Windows Key + I

Select **Change PC Settings.**

Click on **Time and language.**

You can now select your time zone from the drop down menu:

Time

12:34, 23 April 2013

(UTC) Dublin, Edinburgh, Lisbon, London	⌄

Adjust for daylight saving time automatically

On

Change your account picture

You can change your account picture by pressing the keyboard shortcut:

Windows Key + I

Select **Change PC Settings.**

Click on the **Accounts** item and then **Your account.**

You can now use the **Browse** button to find an image to use, or, if you have a camera built into your computer, you'll see the camera button in the **Create an account picture** section.   Just click that and take your account photo.

NOTE: To change the image on an account, you need to be logged into that account. You can easily switch accounts by clicking the desktop/taskbar and then pressing the keyboard shortcut **ALT + F4.**   You can then select the option to **"Switch User".**

Connecting to a WIFI

Whenever you connect to a "new" WIFI, you need to enter a password. This password will be remembered, so you only need to enter it the once.

To connect to a WIFI, press the keyboard shortcut:

Windows Key + I

Then click the **Networks** icon:

The Networks sidebar appears.

Any networks that are detected appear in the WIFI list. Click the one you want to connect to.

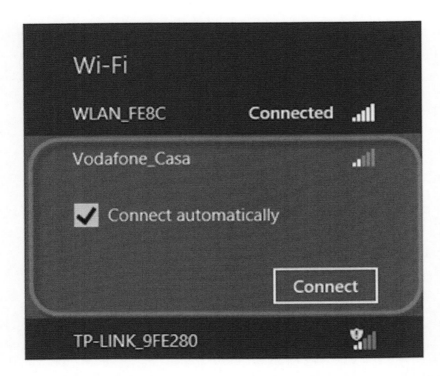

Click the **Connect** button that appears, and enter your password or "network security key" for that network.

You will then be connected.

Another way to get to the Network settings is to click on the Networks icon in the taskbar.

Then connect as above.

Change the Windows 8 language

Unlike some previous versions of Windows, you can change the Windows 8 language without having to buy an expansion pack (or whole new copy of the operating system). You will have to download a language pack though, so you do need to be connected to the Internet.

To do this, press the keyboard shortcut:

Windows Key + I

Select **Change PC Settings**.

Click on the **Time and Language**, then **Region and language**.

Click **Add a language**.

Select the language from those listed and click on OK. If there is more than one variation of the language, you will need to choose the one you want, i.e. English (United Kingdom), English (United States).

Next click the **Add** button to add the language.   It will now appear in your list of languages.   Click on it to open a menu:

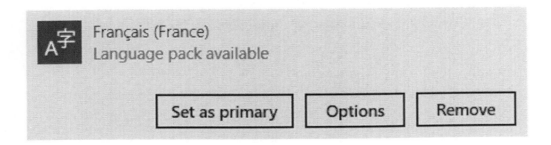

There is an **Options** link.   Click it.

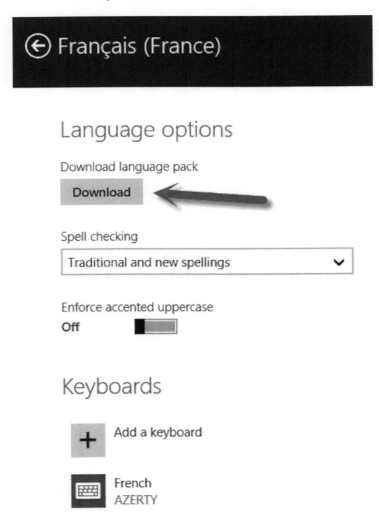

Click the link to **Download** language pack.

The language will now be downloaded and installed, but you are not quite done yet. Click the language in the list, and select **Set as Primary**.

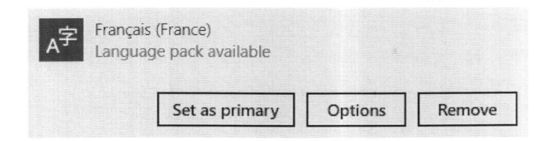

You'll need to restart your computer (or at least log out and back in again), for the changes to take place.   When you do, Windows 8 will be in your newly installed language.

Using dual monitors

Windows 8 has good support for multiple monitors.

The first thing you need to do is identify the available "video" ports on your computer. These can be DVI, VGA or HDMI ports. If you have the option of using an HDMI port (High Definition Multimedia Interface), then use this one.

Plug your second monitor into your computer using an appropriate cable.

Windows 8 will automatically detect the second monitor.

Press the keyboard shortcut **Windows Key + K**, to bring up the devices bar.

You'll see a link to **Second Screen.** Click it to bring up the configuration settings. You have a few options that will decide how the second screen will be used:

PC screen only - Blanks out the second monitor to only show the primary screen.

Duplicate - You see the same desktop on both monitors.

Extend - Essentially gives you two desktops to work with as the screen real estate is extended over both monitors.

Second screen only - Blanks out the primary monitor so you only use the second screen.

Most people will probably choose extend as it means you'll have more room to work with for your open applications.

NOTE: When using "extend", traditional Windows applications can be moved onto both screens by dragging them from one monitor to the other. However, Metro apps behave a little differently. You can drag these from one monitor to another like so:

Position the mouse at the top of the screen until the cursor changes to a hand. Next grab and drag the app down a fraction to "undock" it. Now you can move it across to the other monitor.

Fortunately there is also a keyboard shortcut to move a Metro app across more easily:

Windows Key + PageUp/PageDown

The position of the second monitor in "Extend" mode

When your monitors "extend" the desktop, Windows 8 needs to know where the second monitor is positioned on your desk, so that it knows which edges of the two monitors are joined. To set this up, press the keyboard shortcut:

Windows Key + W

This brings up the **Settings** search screen.

Start typing "resolution" until you see **Adjust screen resolution**.

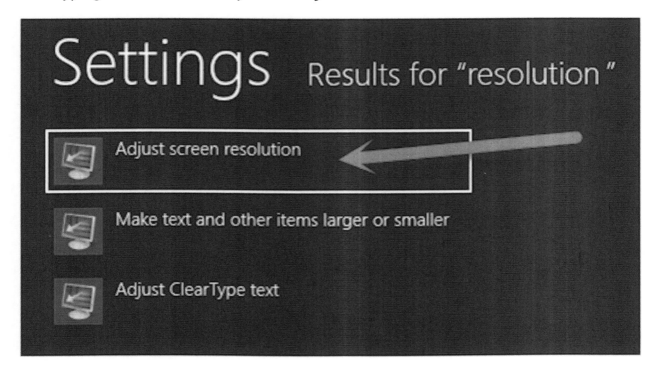

Click it to open the settings.

The image of the two monitors at the top of this screen represents the physical positions of my two monitors.

My laptop monitor is (1), and my second monitor is (2).   In my office, my second monitor is physically positioned above the laptop monitor, and since that is how I have it set up in Windows, I can drag items directly up, or down, to move items between the monitors.   This diagram therefore tells Windows which edges of your monitors are connected in the extended desktop.

You need to place the monitors in this diagram to match how you physically have them located in your workspace.   You can rearrange this diagram simply by dragging the monitor images into position.

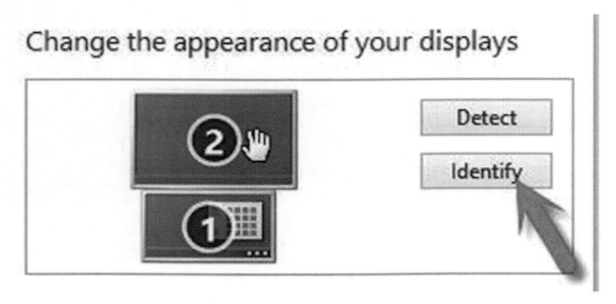

Change the appearance of your displays

Move your mouse over the monitor icons and the cursor changes to a hand.   Click and grab (hold down), the left mouse button, and then drag them into the correct position.

NOTE: If for any reason you are unsure which monitor is which, click the **Identify** button.   This will place a large number 1 and 2 on your physical monitors.

Reinstall Windows 8

If you need to reinstall Windows 8, it's very easy. Press the keyboard shortcut:

Windows Key + I

Click on **Change PC Settings**.

Click on the **Update and Recovery** and then **Recovery**.

Remove everything and reinstall Windows

If you want to recycle your PC or completely start again, you can reset it to its factory settings.

Get started

Click the **Get Started** button and follow the instructions.

WARNING: This will remove all of your programs and files, and return your PC back to the factory settings. If you need to save any files, make sure you back them up to a separate storage device before reinstalling Windows.

How to refresh your computer

If your computer starts to slow down, you can refresh it. Basically this cleans up the installation without removing your personal documents. However, this isn't the dream feature PC and Laptop users having been waiting for. See the notes at the end of this section to find out why.

To refresh your computer press the keyboard shortcut:

Windows Key + I

Click **Change PC Settings.**

Click on the **Update and Recovery** and then **Recovery**.

Refresh your PC without affecting your files

If your PC isn't running well, you can refresh it without losing your photos, music, videos and other personal files.

Get started

Click the **Get started** button and follow instructions on the screen.

Notes on Refreshing your PC:

1. Your files and personalisation settings won't change.
2. PC Settings are restored to defaults.
3. Metro apps from the Windows Store will not be touched.
4. Traditional Windows applications will be removed.
5. You will get a list of removed apps saved to your desktop.

As you can see, this is a better feature for tablet and phone users than it is for PC users.

Emails - setting up an email address in Windows Mail

To be honest, if you are a heavy email user, I'd recommend you use a Windows Application rather than the built in Metro version of Mail. Metro Mail is a little lightweight.

A great free email client is Thunderbird from Mozilla:

https://www.mozilla.org/EN/thunderbird/

For those that want to use Windows Mail, let me show you how to set up an email address.

The first thing you need to realise about Windows Mail is that it can only work with iMAP email accounts. Most web hosts offer both POP3 and iMAP, so check for the settings with your host to get your iMAP settings.

Gmail also offers iMAP settings.

I'll set up a Gmail email address first and then show you how to manually set up an account.

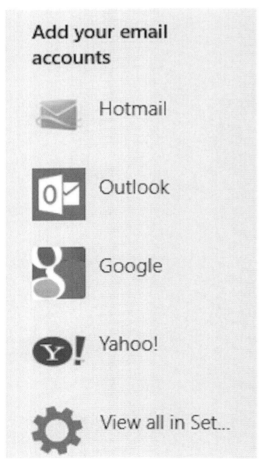

To access Windows Mail, open the start screen **(Windows key)**.

If you have a Windows Mail tile visible, click it. Otherwise start typing "mail" and you'll find it.

Open Windows Mail.

If this is the first email you are setting up in Windows Mail, you'll see a menu in the bottom left of the screen, asking what type of email address you are setting up.

You'll see an option for most of the free email providers. I'll choose the Google option in a moment. However, before I do, perhaps you might want to set up a different type of email address not in the list. To do this, you need to click the bottom option **"View all in Set..."** This will open a bar on the right, offering the option for "Other Account". We'll look at that in a moment.

153

NOTE: I have had problems connecting to Gmail accounts in the past, even though they are directly supported. If you have a problem, then use the "Other Account" option and set it up manually.

OK, to set up the Gmail address, click the **Google** button.

Enter your Google email address and password, and click **Connect**.

That's it! If everything goes to plan, the email account will be created in Windows Mail.

NOTE: If you have 2-step verification set up on your Google account, you will need to go in and generate a password specifically to use with Windows Mail. If you have no idea what I have just said, don't worry. Chances are you are not using 2-step verification.

Adding a second email address to Windows Mail

When you have one email added, there is no obvious way to add a second account. To do this, you need to open the Charms bar (**Windows key + C**, or mouse top right then vertically down).

In the Charms bar, click on the **Setting** button at the bottom.

Under Settings, click **Accounts**.

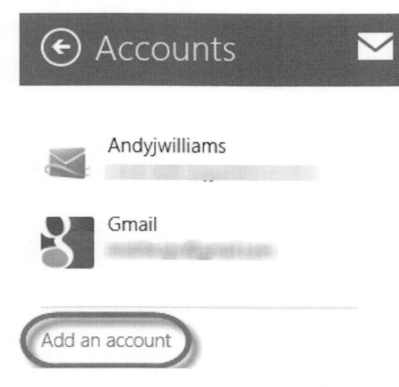

Click on **Add an account.**

You can then add an account as shown earlier.

Manually setting up an email account

If you need to manually add an email account, choose to add an "**Other Account**".

You'll be asked whether you want to connect using Exchange Activesync or IMAP. Most people will choose **IMAP**, so select that option and click the **Connect** button.

You will then be asked to enter your email address and password.

Enter them and click **Connect.**

Windows Mail will try to fill in the settings if it recognises the domain in the email address.   If this fails, you'll be prompted with a screen to enter your details manually:

Email address

Username

Password

Incoming (IMAP) email server   Port

                                                                   993

☑ Incoming server requires SSL

Outgoing (SMTP) email server   Port

                                                                   465

☑ Outgoing server requires SSL

☑ Outgoing server requires authentication

☑ Use the same username and password to send and receive email

Connect   Cancel

You'll need to enter email address, login username and password.

Next up is the IMAP server (incoming mail).   You get this from your web host.   IMAP usually uses port 993, so unless your host tells you otherwise, leave that as it is.

Outgoing email uses an SMTP server, and again, your web host will give you that. Enter it.

The other settings related to security and authentication should be correct, but do check with your web host if you find that the default settings don't work.

Once you've entered the details, click the **Connect** button to add the email account. If all the details are correct, the email address should be added.

Change email account name in Windows Mail

You may want to change the email account name in Windows Mail.

To do this, open Mail.

Open the Charms bar (**Windows Key + C** or mouse top right then vertically down) and select **Settings.**

Select **Accounts.**

Now click on the email address that you want to edit.   The settings will open.

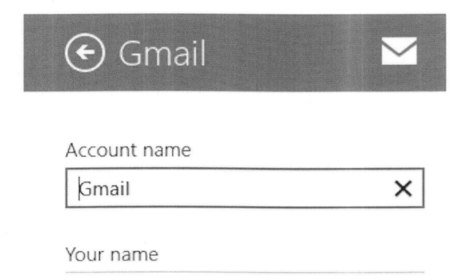

The top box allows you to edit the account name.   Once changed, it is automatically saved, so just close the sidebar.

Getting notifications when new Mail arrives

You can get notifications when new Windows Mail arrives, but this feature may not be set up by default.

Open Windows Mail (go to the start screen and click on the Mail tile, or start typing "Mail" to find it).

Press the shortcut key: Windows Key + C

Choose **Settings** from the Charms bar.

Click **Accounts**.

Select the email account you want notifications for.

Scroll to the bottom of the email account settings.

Show email notifications for this account

On

Click the switch to turn it On.

Now when you get an email, you'll get a visual Windows notification.

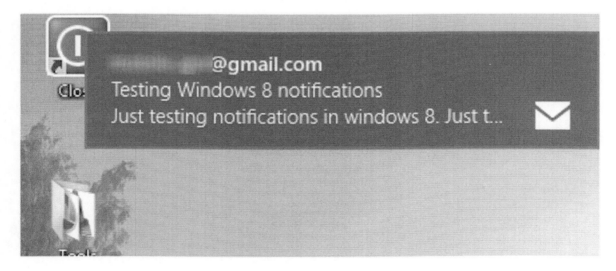

Windows 8 keyboard shortcuts

Windows Key   Show start screen

Windows Key + D   Show Desktop

Windows Key + ,   Previews the Desktop while you are
                                    holding the keys

Charms bar shortcuts
Windows Key + C   Charms Menu
Windows Key + Q   Charms Menu Search
Windows Key + H   Charms Menu Share
Windows Key + K   Charms Menu Devices
Windows Key + I   Charms Menu Settings

Search shortcuts
Windows Key   to open the start screen, then start
                                    typing to search

Windows Key + Q   Search Everywhere
Windows Key + F   Search Files
Windows Key + W   Search Settings

Find open apps
Windows Key + Tab   Scroll through Open Metro applications
Windows Key + SHIFT + Tab   Scroll in reverse order
ALT + Tab   Scroll through all open apps (Metro +
                                    Windows applications)

Snapping apps to the sidebar
Windows Key + .   Snap the app to the right sidebar, but
                                    press again to snap to the left and again
                                    to unsnap

Windows Key + SHIFT + .   Snap the app to the left, then the right
                                    then unsnap

Zooming in and out
CTRL + Mouse Scroll wheel   Zoom in/out

CTRL + +/-   Zoom in/out
Windows Key + +/-   Zoom in/out using magnifier
Windows Key + ESCAPE   Exit the magnifier

Controlling Metro apps
Windows Key + Z or **right mouse**   Show App Commands / Menu

button
Windows Key + F4	Close App with focus (Metro apps and Traditional Windows applications).
Windows Key + E	Launch File Explorer
Windows Key + L	Lock PC (goes to the lock screen)
Windows Key + T	Cycles through taskbar icons. Press enter to launch one of them
Windows Key + X	Opens the advanced Windows Settings menu from bottom left of the screen
Windows Key + PAGE UP/DOWN	When start screen is open, this moves the start screen to a second monitor

Minimize & Maximize Windows

Windows Key + M	Minimize all windows
Windows Key + SHIFT + M	Restore minimized Windows
Windows Key + R	Opens the Run dialog box
Windows Key + Up Arrow	Maximize current window
Windows Key + Down Arrow	Minimize current window
Windows Key + Right Arrow	Maximize on the right of the screen
Windows Key + Left Arrow	Maximize on the left of screen
CTRL + SHIFT + ESCAPE	Open Task Manager
Windows Key + Print Screen	Captures a screenshot of your desktop and saves to the Pictures/Screenshots folder
Windows Key + Pause Break	Opens the system properties screen
SHIFT + DELETE	Permanently deletes a file without sending to the recycle bin
Windows Key + F1	Opens Windows Help & Support
Windows Key + 0 .. 9	Opens the corresponding taskbar application. If it is already open, then bring it to the front.
Windows Key + P	Secondary display modes for those with dual monitors
Windows Key + U	Opens Windows Ease of Access Center
Windows Key + Spacebar	Switch between installed language and keyboard layouts
Windows Key + Enter	Open the Narrator

Copy / Paste, Redo & Undo

CTRL + C	Copy selected item(s)

CTRL + X	Cut the selected item(s)
CTRL + V	Paste Item(s)
CTRL + Z	Undo the last action
CTRL + Y	Redo the last action

Where to go from here

Firstly, I hope you have enjoyed this book.   If you have a moment, I'd love it if you could leave a review on Amazon.

You can find "Migrating to Windows 8" on:

Amazon.com: http://www.amazon.com/dp/B00CJ8AD9E

Amazon.co.uk: https://www.amazon.co.uk/dp/B00CJ8AD9E

For other Amazon stores, search for: **B00CJ8AD9E**

NOTE:

This book is available as both a physical book and a Kindle book. Both versions can be found on Amazon using the links above.   Just switch between the two options – Kindle and paperback.

A cheat sheet

You should have a really good grasp of Windows 8 by now, but the best way of consolidating your knowledge is to keep using your computer.   I'd highly recommend you create a 'cheat sheet' to keep by your computer, with a list of the keyboard shortcuts that you find most useful.

"How to" suggestions?

If you have any suggestions for the "How to" section of this book, please email me at:

migratingw8@gmail.com

I'll include the best suggestions in future updates to this book.

My Other Kindle Books

Kindle Publishing - Format, Publish & Promote your Books on Kindle

Why Publish on Amazon Kindle?

Kindle publishing has captured the imagination of aspiring writers. Now, more than at any other time in our history, an opportunity is knocking. Getting your books published no longer means sending out hundreds of letters to publishers and agents. It no longer means getting hundreds of rejection letters back. Today, you can write and publish your own books on Amazon Kindle without an agent or publisher.

Is it really possible to make a good income as an Indie author?

The fact that you are reading this book description tells me you are interested in publishing your own material on Kindle. You may have been lured here by promises of quick riches. Well, I have good news and bad. The bad news is that publishing and profiting from Kindle takes work and dedication. Don't just expect to throw up sub-par material and make a killing in sales. You need to produce good stuff to be successful at this. The good news is that you can make a very decent living from writing and publishing for Kindle.

My own success with Kindle publishing

As I explain at the beginning of this book, I published my first Kindle book in August 2012, yet by December 2012, just 5 months later, I was making what many people consider to be a full time income. As part of my own learning experience, I setup a Facebook page in July 2012 to share my Kindle publishing journey (there is a link to the Facebook page inside this book). On that Facebook page, I shared the details of what I did, problems I needed to overcome, I shared my growing income reports, and most of all, I offered help to those who asked for it. What I found was a huge and growing audience for this type of education, and ultimately, that's why I wrote this book.

What's in this book?

This book covers what I have learned on my journey and what has worked for me. I have included sections to answer the questions I myself asked, as well as those questions people asked me. This book is a complete reference manual for successfully formatting, publishing & promoting your books on Amazon Kindle. There is even a section for non-US publishers because there is stuff you specifically need to know.

I see enormous potential in Kindle Publishing and in 2013, I intend to grow this side of my own business. Kindle publishing has been liberating for me and I am sure it will be for you too.

Search Amazon for **B00BEIX34C**

WordPress For Beginners

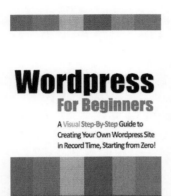

Do you want to build a website but scared it's too difficult?

Building a website was once the domain of computer geeks. Not anymore. WordPress makes it possible for anyone to create and run a professional looking website

While WordPress is an amazing tool, the truth is it does have a steep learning curve, even if you have built websites before. Therefore, the goal of this book is to take anyone, even a complete beginner, and get them building a professional looking website. I'll hold your hand, step-by-step, all the way.

As I was planning this book, I made one decision early on. I wanted to use screenshots of everything, so the reader wasn't left looking for something on their screen that I was describing in text. This book has screenshots. I haven't counted them all, but it must be close to 300. These screenshots will help you find the things I am talking about. They'll help you check your settings and options against a screenshot of mine. You look, compare, and move on to the next section.

With so many screenshots, you may be worried that the text might be a little on the skimpy side. No need to worry there. I have described every step of your journey in great detail. In all, this book has over 35,000 words.

This book will surely cut your learning curve associated with WordPress

Every chapter of the book ends with a "Tasks to Complete" section. By completing these tasks, you'll not only become proficient at using WordPress, you'll become confident & enjoy using WordPress too.

Search Amazon for **B009ZVO3H6**

CSS For Beginners

Learn CSS with detailed instructions, step-by-step screenshots and video tutorials showing CSS in action on real sites.

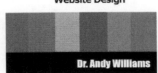

Most websites you visit use Cascading Style Sheets (CSS) for everything, from font selection & formatting to layout & design. Whether you are building WordPress sites or traditional HTML websites, this book aims to take the complete beginner to a level where they are comfortable digging into the CSS code and making changes to their own projects. CSS for Beginners will show you how to make all these formatting & layout changes in easy to understand steps.

The book covers the following topics:

- Why CSS is important
- Classes, Pseudo Classes, Pseudo Elements & IDs

- The Float Property
- Units of Length
- Using DIVs
- Tableless Layouts, including how to create 2-column and 3-column layouts
- The Box Model
- Creating Menus with CSS
- Images & Background Images

The hands on approach of this book will get YOU building your own Style Sheets. Also included in this book:

- Over 160 screenshots and 20,000 words detailing every step you need to take
- Full source code for all examples shown
- Video Tutorials

The video tutorials accompanying this book show you:

- How to investigate the HTML & CSS behind any website.
- How to experiment with your own design in real time, and only make the changes permanent on your site when you are ready to implement them.

Note: A basic knowledge of HTML is recommended, although all source code from the book can be downloaded and used as you work through the book

Search Amazon for **B00AFV44NS**

Printed in Great Britain
by Amazon.co.uk, Ltd.,
Marston Gate.